The Beginner's Guide
To Teaching with Words in Color

American English Edition

Educational Solutions Worldwide Inc.

Copyright © 2009 Educational Solutions Worldwide Inc.
First Edition
Based on the works of Dr. Caleb Gattegno, including: Notes For Parents, ©1979
Compiled by Educational Solutions Worldwide Inc.
All rights reserved
ISBN 978-0-87825-063-9

Educational Solutions Worldwide Inc.
2nd Floor 99 University Place, New York, N.Y. 10003-4555
www.EducationalSolutions.com

Table of Contents

Introduction 1

R_0 The First Group of Activities 17

R_1 The Second Group of Activities 31

R_2, R_3 and Beyond 87

Toolbox of Teaching Techniques and Games 89

Games 109

More Games 119

- 21 color-coded Word Charts (size varies depending on set)
- 1 Fidel phonic code (size varies depending on set)
- Color Key for the American English Fidel
- Reference Guide to the Fidel Phonic Code
- Reading Primers R_0 & R_1
- Reading Primer R_2
- Reading Primer R_3
- Student Workbook 1
- Student Workbook 2
- Book of Stories
- The Beginner's Guide to Teaching with Words in Color
- Collapsible metal pointer

Introduction

Introduction

Words in Color is for teachers and students to teach and learn how to read and write. It has been called unique, advanced, comprehensive, common sense, flexible, stimulating, and fun. We call it an appropriate approach, one that respects the reality of the challenge of teaching and learning how to read and write English.

Written English employs six simple conventions; by introducing these early on, the students often find their efforts are successful. In Words in Color these conventions are inherent in the reading approach and therefore don't need to be learned as a series of rules.

1. Words are printed or written on a straight line.

2. We read from left to right.

3. Words are printed with spaces between them. The spaces do not match the way we pause or run our words together in speech, so we usually ignore the spaces when we read aloud to get the proper rhythm of speech.

4. Sounds are represented by signs. A sign may be a single letter, or a combination of letters.

5. In print, the signs can be switched around to form different words, just as sounds can be reordered to form different spoken words. (pat, tap, apt). We see this property of words as a form of algebra that can be easily mastered.

6. Reading should have the same melody that speech has, but the correct melody can only be found after the meaning of the whole phrase has been grasped.

Characteristics of the Approach

Students begin with color-coded vowels and combinations of vowels, which are decoded by reading aloud. Then they move on to syllables and combinations into words, and then to combinations of words into simple and increasingly more complex sentences. In parallel, students use their Primer Books R_0 & R_1, R_2, R_3 and Workbooks 1 & 2 to consolidate their work done with the charts by reading aloud and writing. Game like activities provide an intellectual climate that keeps the student's interest in words and their alertness at a high level.

As the student becomes proficient, the stress is shifted from reading words to understanding what is read; then, to the study of the phonetics, spelling, grammar, and on to creative writing.

Effective and Efficient use of Time

In this approach, we try to make the most effective and efficient use of time so that the student learns to read in the minimum time possible and is, while learning, being educated in the fullest sense.

To achieve this effectiveness and efficiency, **drill and repetition are banned** from the start and are replaced by game-like activities which on the one hand provide the motivation for learning, and on the other hand give the student the opportunity to form pictures in their mind which can be recalled easily. This results in a tremendous acceleration of the learning process of reading and writing.

Autonomy & Responsibility

At the same time students learn to correct their own mistakes. The student will be asked to seriously play a number of games, each game having a particular function, complementary to that of the others. Together these games will give students the opportunity to meet and overcome all the challenges of reading and writing, without being told any answers. The games proposed here are original and proven effective.

Memorization Takes a Back Seat

Another characteristic of the approach is its deliberate reduction of the need for memorization. Instead, the emphasis is on consciousness and recognition. When students see something in front of them, and come to conclusions themselves, they retain that knowledge without memorizing.

Natural Ways of Learning

Reading is concerned with a set of conventions that follow historically developed rules making this a highly intellectual activity. We have seen time and time again that young children, and even very young children, are more than capable of operating at or beyond the level needed for success.

Methods in this guide are similar to those used spontaneously by children whenever they learn independently of adults in essential fields of experience. An example of this is when a child learns to walk; a parent does not have to tell the child to put one foot in front of another. Instead, the child learns through observation and experimentation. Respect for children's natural ways of learning is inherent in this approach.

Self Discovery and Focus

With Words in Color, the student has the opportunity to discover how our language works for themselves, and in doing so becomes responsible for their own learning. In addition, because of the way in which challenges are formulated and presented, students can use multiple ways of thinking and operate at a high intellectual level. When a challenge is presented, students are asked thought provoking questions that lead them to an awareness about the activity (ex. that red letters are all pronounced the same, regardless of the shape or combination).

Overview of the Materials

The American English Fidel™

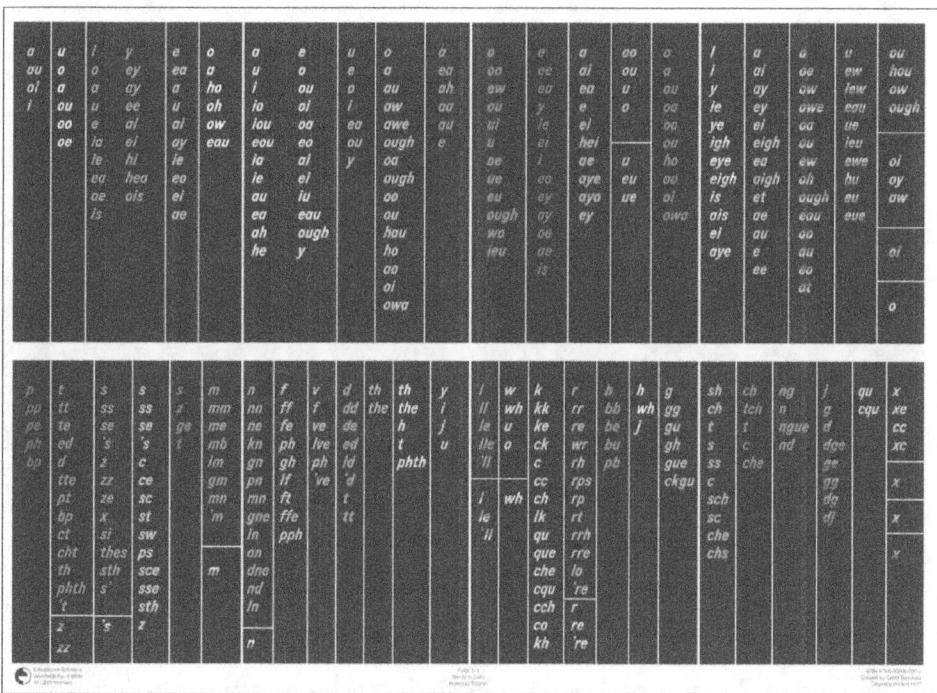

The American English Fidel ™ is your guide through the language. The Fidel, an Ethiopian word meaning syllabary, presents all the 400+ ways of spelling the sounds in English. Color is applied to help beginning readers know how to read a word. For example, when we apply color to the words fr<u>ui</u>t, fl<u>u</u>, and f<u>oo</u>d, we provide conditions that enable students to become aware that in this case <u>ui</u>, <u>u</u>, and <u>oo</u> (in dark green) are all to be read with the same sound, even though the spellings are different.

On the Fidel, the most common spellings of each sound are located at the top of each column. As you go down the column, the spellings become increasingly more rare.

The 21 Color-coded Word Charts

Chart #'s 4 – 8 of the set of 21 color-coded Word Charts

A graded set of 21 colored word charts introduces students through carefully selected examples to the spectrum of spellings for each sound, and how to decode them. The words chosen at each level are first those most useful in sentence formation and progress from easier, to common usage, to difficult and uncommon examples.

The Reading Primers – R_0 & R_1, R_2, R_3

The student Reading Primers introduce in stages all the different spellings and sounds of American English, giving examples of words, and of their use in sentences. They are printed in black and white and are written for use in conjunction with the Fidel ™ and the Words in Color set of 21 Word Charts. They provide a detailed progression for classroom and home work and eliminate the dependence on color for reading.

The Workbooks - 1 & 2, and The Book of Stories

Student Workbooks 1 & 2

Each Workbook contains 7 multi-page worksheets with graduated questions and exercises to consolidate the reading skills at each stage. They provide a program of individual study where imagination and creativity are encouraged, with a proven framework for their expression. The worksheets progress from the beginning of reading and writing through to an introductory study of grammar.

Book of Stories

Specially written for use with Words in Color, 40 stories describe events in the daily lives of an everyday family. As the first continuous reading material students meet, this book takes into account the increasing complexity of written English as presented on the Fidel, the set of 21 color-coded Word Charts, and the Reading Primers.

Reference Materials for the Fidel

Reference Guide To The Fidel Phonic Code

This is a comprehensive resource that presents sample words and their corresponding locations on the Word Charts for every sound and spelling on the Fidel.

Color Key for the American English Fidel

This is a quick reference for use with the Fidel of all the sounds and spellings of English.

The Beginner's Guide to Teaching with Words in Color

The Beginners Guide To Teaching With Words in Color is for teachers and parents who are new to the approach. This guide provides a general introduction to the materials, and the takes the first time instructor through R_0 and R_1. It also provides a toolbox of games and teaching techniques that can be used at any stage.

Additional Resources

Visit the Words in Color section at www.EducationalSolutions.com for updates, instructional videos, and additional resources on how to use and apply Words in Color.

How to use this Beginner's Guide

This guide is broken up into four major sections:

1. This introductory section

2. A step-by-step guide to R_0 The First Group of Activities, arranged by table number and activity number

3. A step-by-step guide to R_1 The Second Group of Activities, arranged by table number and activity number

4. A Toolbox of Teaching Techniques and Games

The Toolbox can also be referred to by the teacher as you progress to R_2 and R_3.

For additional materials and how use Words in Color, please visit the Words in Color Section of www.EducationalSolutions.com.

Do I have to start from the beginning if my student already has some reading skills?

It is not necessary, however, some users have found that when you start from the first lessons, students start to understand the foundations of the English language. More challenging words will become easier to read and spell since they have the inherent knowledge. It has been found that the pace of learning in subsequent lessons is often accelerated when you start from the beginning.

Regional Dialects and Pronunciation Differences

The pronunciations of words chosen for Words in Color are consistent with those as presented in The American Heritage Dictionary, Fourth Edition. However, we understand there are many regional dialects of American English and that each region of the continent has its own way of pronouncing certain sounds. For example, the sign o in the word pop found in Chart 1 may be pronounced differently by someone in Boston,

Massachusetts versus someone in Dallas, Texas and someone in Minneapolis, Minnesota. And this may be different again from the form of English spoken in Chicago, Illinois.

We encourage you to pronounce the sounds (and their associated color) as you normally would. In fact, depending on the region you live in, there may be no distinction between the pronunciations associated with certain colors. For example, the o (colored white) as in the word pop and the o (colored ochre) as in the word off may be pronounced the same in the dialect of English spoken where you live.

By all means, use the dialect of English that you use naturally. This program is about learning to read, not learning to pronounce. Treat this an opportunity to explore the richness of the English language – one that has taken centuries to develop.

Where are the capital letters? Is this a mistake?

Capital letters and punctuation have intentionally been omitted for the beginning stages of reading and writing. If your child or student already knows about capitals, then they will automatically apply that knowledge. If they do not know about these conventions, it is better to wait until they have a grasp of the basics before complicating matters with different shapes (capitals) for the same signs.

How much time should I spend on this at home?

Introducing a sound, or playing a game can take just two minutes. You can keep playing the games and increasing the challenges for as long as your student is interested. For very young children, you may find you have more success if you use Words in Color more frequently, but for shorter periods of time. Be aware of the interest level in your student; if they are ready to do something else after five minutes, then five minutes is enough. If they are very interested in a game, keep playing and keep increasing the challenge. If you spend one hour on an activity, and the student is only interested for 20 minutes, then 40 minutes of the lesson may not have been effective. Think quality, not quantity.

Teachers and Parents: Before You Begin

Getting to Know the Fidel™ Phonic Code

Take the full color version of your Fidel, and examine it for the following.

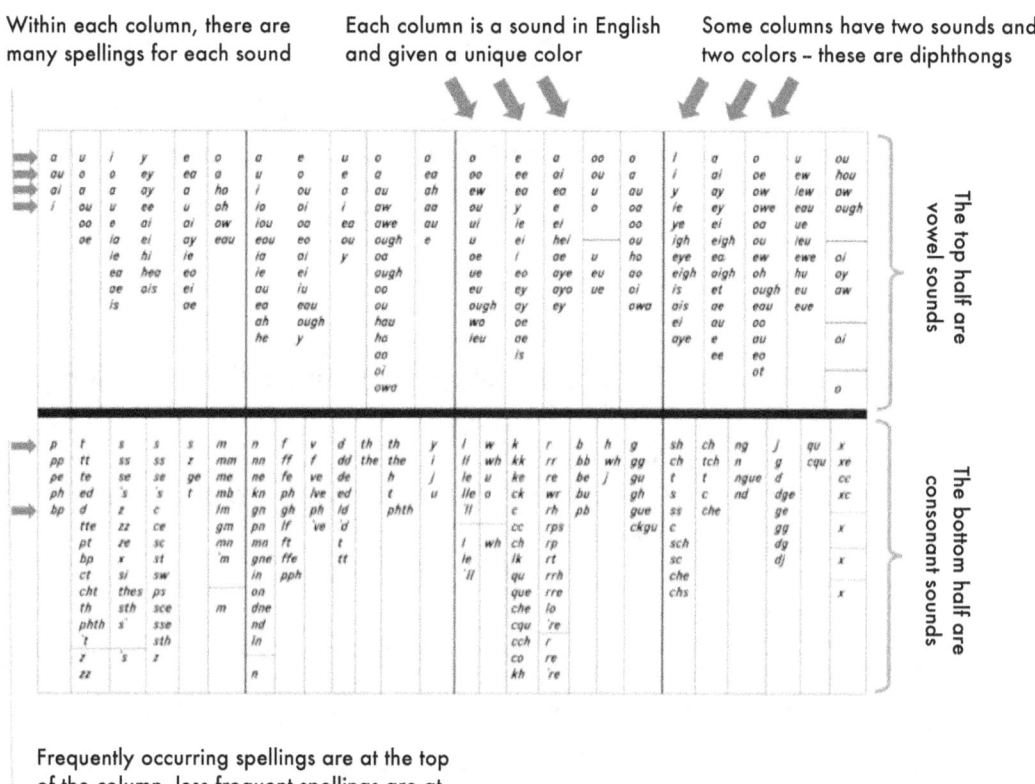

Within each column, there are many spellings for each sound

Each column is a sound in English and given a unique color

Some columns have two sounds and two colors – these are diphthongs

Frequently occurring spellings are at the top of the column, less frequent spellings are at

Refer to the Reference Guide to the Fidel Phonic Code and the Color Key for the American English Fidel for spellings, sounds, and sample words.

Getting to Know English Spellings & Sounds

The following activities are designed to make you more familiar with the use of the materials. We have found that going through these activities, in whole or in part is very beneficial for the teacher. It is not necessary to complete each one before you begin. You can always return to these as you progress.

Activity 1

Start at Word Chart #1, for each word on the first row, say it and:

- Find the matching color and spelling on the Fidel™ Phonic Code
- Continue until you have finished all the words on the row
- Repeat the process for the next line

Activity 2

Start at the first sound/spelling on the top left of the Fidel Phonic Code.

- For each sound/spelling:
  Can you find any/all instances of its use on the word charts?
  How many did you find?

Activity 3

In each Reading Primer (R_0 & R_1, R_2, R_3), find the Word Building Tables 0-7. Starting with Table 1, find the corresponding sounds and spellings on the Fidel Phonic Code. After you have finished, proceed to the next Word Building Table.

Activity 4

Starting with Reading Primer R_0 & R_1, read each word and sentence. Can you find words in the Reading Primer book that are also written on the Word Charts? After you have finished one Reading Primer, proceed to the next.

Activity 5

Starting with Worksheet 1 in Student Workbook 1:

- Identify the spellings and sounds that are in use.
- Find the corresponding locations for the sounds and spellings on the Fidel

R_0
The First Group of Activities

Activities for R₀ Table 0

In the R₀ portion of Reading Primers R₀ & R₁ you will work on the following sounds:

a	u	i	e	o

This initial table is made of five vowel sounds:

- a as in at
- u as in up
- i as in it
- e as in pet
- o as in pot

At this stage you will also be making your student aware of some conventions of written English:

- The text is to be read from left to right
- There are spaces between the words
- Letters, alone, or in groups represent sounds

Keep in mind, you won't tell the student these conventions. Let them discover for themself.

Table 0.1 Activity 1

Sound / Spelling
- a as in p<u>a</u>t

Materials
- Chart 0
- Reading Primers R_0 & R_1
- Pointer

Beginning Notes

In our approach to teaching reading, we refer to sounds and not letters. The rationale is that there are only 26 letters in English, but they produce 59 sounds. Combinations of the 5 vowels alone create 23 sounds with hundreds of spellings – this is a great source of confusion for learners. Using the name of a letter creates an incomplete notion of the letter's pronunciation, and makes it difficult for learners to accept new spellings.

Rather than refer to letters, we refer to sounds. For example, the sound associated with p as in p<u>a</u>t can be referred to by the sound/color chestnut, and s as in u<u>s</u> can be called lime green. Refer to the Reference Guide to the Fidel Phonic Code for a complete list of names for all 59 sounds.

If you give the time and support for your child or student to work through and conquer the challenges presented, they will become better prepared to meet even bigger, more complex challenges. Remember:

- Resist the temptation to give answers.
- Allow your student time to work through and conquer challenges.
- Repetition can be detrimental to the learning process. Thus, try to mix up the challenges if your student is "not getting it."
- If difficulties arise, revert back to what is already known and go from there.

Table 0.1 Activity 1

Steps

a

- Using your pointer, point to a on Chart 0 and say its sound once. Remember you are not naming a letter of the alphabet, you are using the sound a as in pat.

- Point to another a and ask your student to say the sound

- Point to each sign in "aa" and ask your student to say the sounds. If they cannot say these sounds then say it once and ask them to say it.

- Point to each spelling (sign) in "aaa" and ask your student to say the sounds. If they cannot say these sounds then say it once and ask them to say it.

- Switch to Reading Primers R_0 & R_1. Point to a sign a and ask your student: "How would you say this one?"

- Continue pointing (without speaking), giving your student the opportunity to say the sound and to listen to themselves saying it. Spend only a few minutes on this, just the time required for your student to be sure which sound is associated with the sign a.

- Point to the other "words" on page 6 of Reading Primers R_0 & R_1 groups like aa, aaa, and listen to your student read them. If a difficulty arises, point back to a single a and ask: "What did you say for this one?" then "How many of these do you see in this group?" For example aa, "Say them as fast as possible" because they are close together.

Table 0.1 Activity 1

Teaching Techniques and Games

Visual Dictation:

- Teacher uses the pointer: In Reading Primers R_0 & R_1, or on Chart 0 point to a single <u>a</u> a few times, varying both the number of taps and the rhythm. If for instance you touch <u>a</u> once, pause, and then touch it three times in rapid succession. Your student is likely to say: <u>a</u> (pause) <u>aaa</u>.

- Student uses the pointer: Your student points to a single <u>a</u> a few times, varying both the number of taps and the rhythm and you would produce the sounds to match.

Oral Dictation:

- Student uses the pointer: Teacher would say the "words," and your student would then tap the signs with the same rhythm. For example: if the teacher says <u>a</u> <u>aa</u>, or <u>a</u> <u>aaa</u>, or <u>aa</u> <u>a</u> then your student would tap the corresponding sounds.

Table 0.2 Activity 1

Sound / Spelling
- <u>u</u> as in <u>u</u>p

Materials
- Chart 0
- Reading Primers R_0 & R_1
- Pointer
- Fidel

Beginning Notes

Table 0.2 Activity 1

Steps

a   u

- Using your pointer, point to <u>u</u> on Chart 0 and say its sound once. Remember you are not naming the alphabet, you are using the sound <u>u</u> as in <u>u</u>p.

- Point to another <u>u</u> and ask your student to say the sound.

- Point to each sign in "<u>uu</u>" and ask your student to say the sounds. If they cannot say these sounds then say it once and ask them to say it.

- Point to each sign in "<u>uuu</u>" and ask your student to say the sounds. If they cannot say these sounds then say it once and ask them to say it.

- Switch to Table 0.2 in Reading Primers R_0 & R_1. Point to a sign <u>u</u> and ask your student: "How would you say this one?"

- Continue pointing (without speaking), giving your student the opportunity to say the sound and to listen to themselves saying it.

- Point to the other "words" on page 9 or 10 of Reading Primers R_0 & R_1 (groups like <u>au</u>, <u>uaa</u>), and listen to your student read them; if a difficulty arises, point back to a single <u>u</u> and ask: "What did you say for this one?" then "How many of these do you see in this group?"

- **Note:** When you see <u>au</u> don't say them as in the word <u>au</u>to, <u>a</u> and <u>u</u> are distinct sounds: the <u>a</u> sound as in p<u>a</u>t and <u>u</u> as in <u>u</u>p.

Table 0.2 Activity 1

Teaching Techniques and Games

Point, Show, Engage 1:
- Using the single signs a and u tap in rhythm (for example, aa u) and ask your student:

  - "What did I show?"
  - "What would the reverse of this be?" or "How would you say it backwards?"
  - "Tap it yourself on the Fidel."

Point, Show, Engage 2:
- Point to one of the "words" on page 9 or 10 of Reading Primers R_0 & R_1 and ask your student to read it. Then ask:

  - "What would the reverse of this be?" or "How do you say it backwards?"
  - "Is that written on this page?" yes? no?
  - If yes, "Can you find it and show it to me?"

Table 0.3, 0.4, 0.5 Activity 1

Sound / Spelling
- i as in it
- e as in pet
- o as in pot

Materials
- Chart 0
- Reading Primers R_0 & R_1
- Pointer
- Fidel

Beginning Notes
- We will now introduce the other three tables in R_0. It is a good idea to introduce each sound one at a time.

Table 0.3, 0.4, 0.5 Activity 1

Steps

a	u	i	e	o

- Repeat the process used for <u>a</u> and <u>u</u> and apply it to:

    - <u>i</u> as in <u>i</u>t
    - <u>e</u> as in p<u>e</u>t
    - <u>o</u> as in p<u>o</u>t

- At some point, your student may want to start writing the signs (letters) they know. At this point, **do not worry about legibility or neatness**. Let them write and read back to you what they have written.

- At the top of the Fidel Phonic Chart, show your student the location of the 5 signs with their respective colors (top left of the Fidel). Listed with them are all the other spellings that represent these sounds in English. You do not need at this stage to tell them why there are so many. But if you must, let them repeat the same sound every time you touch any other sign in the same column (and with the same color).

a	u	i	y	e	o		u	o	a	o	e	a	oo	o	l	a	o	u	ou
au	o	a	ey	ea	a		e	o	ea	oo	ee	ea	ou	a	i	ai	oe	ew	hou
ai	a	u	ay	a	ho		o	ou	ah	ew	ea	e	o	u	y	ay	ow	iew	ow
i	ou	e	ee	u	oh		i	oi	aa	ou	y	ei	oo	o	ie	ey	owe	eau	ough
	oo	ia	ai	ai	ow		io	oa	au	ui	ie	hei	ou		ye	ei	oa	ue	
	oe	ie	ei	ay	eau		iou	eo	e	u	ei	ae	ho	u	igh	eigh	ou	ieu	oi
		ea	hi	ie			eou	ai		oe	i	aye	ao	eu	eye	ea	ew	ewe	oy
		ae	hea	eo			ia	ei		ue	eo	ayo	oi	ue	eigh	aigh	oh	hu	aw
		is	ois	ei			ie	iu		eu	ey	ey	owa		is	et	ough	eu	
				ae			au	eau		ough	ay				ais	ae	eau	eue	oi
							ea	ough		wo	oe				ei	au	oo		
							ah	y		ieu	ae				aye	e	au		o
							he				is					ee	eo		
																	ot		

p	t	s	s	s	m	n	f	v	d	th	th	y	l	w	k	r	b	h	g	sh	ch	ng	j	qu	x
pp	tt	ss	ss	z	mm	nn	ff	f	dd	the	the	i	ll	wh	kk	rr	bb	wh	gg	ch	tch	n	g	cqu	xe
pe	te	se	se	ge	me	ne	fe	ve	de		h	j	le	u	ke	re	be	j	gu	t	t	ngue	d		cc
ph	ed	's	's	t	mb	kn	ph	lve	ed		t	u	'll	o	ck	wr	bu		gh	s	c	nd	dge		xc
bp	d	z	c		lm	gn	gh	ph	ld		phth				c	rh	pb		gue	ss	che		ge		
	tte	zz	ce		gm	pn	lf	've	'd				l	wh	cc	rps			ckgu	c			gg		x
	pt	ze	sc		mn	mn	ft		t				le		ch	rp				sch			dg		
	bp	x	st		'm	gne	ffe		tt				'll		lk	rt				sc			dj		x
	ct	si	sw			in	pph								qu	rrh				che					
	cht	thes	ps		m	on									que	rre				chs					x
	th	sth	sce			dne									cqu	lo									
	phth	s'	sse			ln									cch	're									
	't		sth			n									co	r									
	z	's	z												kh	re									
	zz															're									

Table 0.3, 0.4, 0.5 Activity 1

Teaching Techniques and Games

Oral Dictation:

Teacher says a "word" (<u>aiio</u>) or a "sentence" (<u>aai</u> <u>uu</u> <u>oei</u>) and your student then:

- option 1: Finds the word and points to it
- option 2: Taps out the word or sentence
- option 3: Writes the word or sentence

Visual Dictation:

Teacher taps out a "word," for example <u>eeoa</u> or a "sentence" for example, <u>ea</u> <u>iea</u> <u>aoie</u>

- Student says the word or sentence, then
- Student writes the word or sentence
- Teacher asks "What would the reverse of this be?"
- Teacher asks "Tap it yourself on the Fidel."

Congratulations On Completing R_0

You have now introduced 5 basic vowel sounds.

a	u	i	e	o	

We have also introduced you to a few games and techniques that you will be using throughout Words in Color. Before you progress to R_1, it is suggested you not progress further until your student feels comfortable in combining the various sounds and spellings introduced.

Take as much time as you like to practice and play around with the games and techniques we have presented.

For more tips please visit the Words in Color section at www.EducationalSolutions.com.

R_1
The Second Group of Activities

Word Building Table 1

At the beginning of R₁ (see page 27 of the Reading Primers R₀ & R₁) you will find Word Building Table 1.

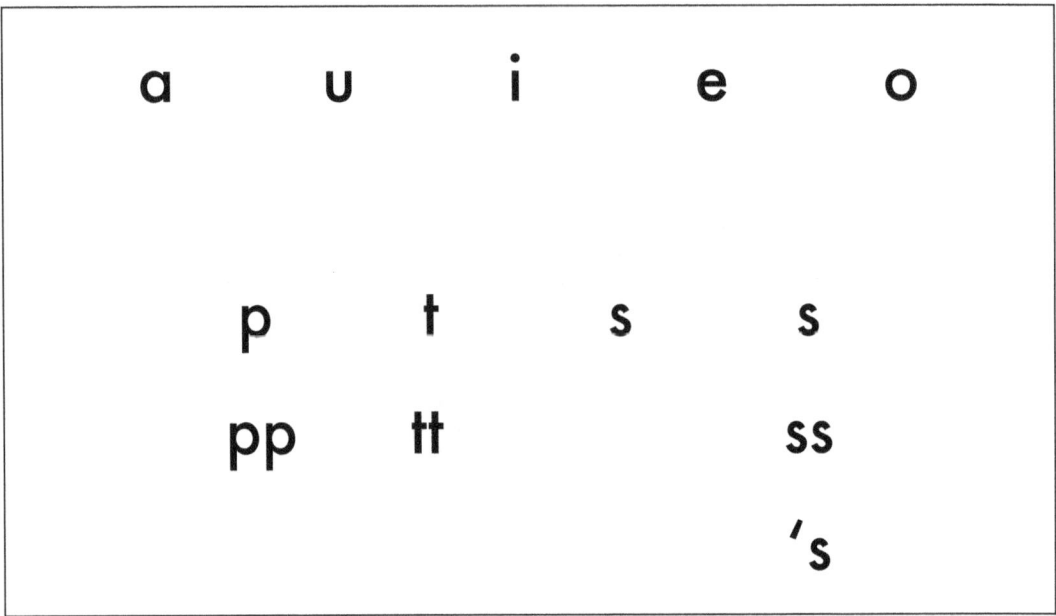

Word Building Table 1.0

This table is made of the five vowels studied in R₀ and introduces four new consonant sounds, with eight different spellings in all.

- The p and pp consonant, pronounced as in the word pat
- The t and tt consonant, pronounced as in the word tap
- The s consonant, pronounced as in the words is, and
- The s, ss, and 's consonants, pronounced as in the words us, pass, or it's

Word Building Table 1

Notes Before you Begin R₁:

- The s appears twice on that page. This is because its sounds differently in is and in us.

- In English, consonants are never spoken in isolation; they are always combined with other sounds – the vowels. Take special care to always combine them with vowels to make syllables that can be spoken.
    - For example, we can't say "p" alone, because it sounds as air passing through our lips with no voice. Instead we always combine it with a vowel sound – pa, pu, etc. Since you can not pronounce a consonant in isolation, always combine it with a vowel sound, and pronounce it as a single sound. Vowels placed next to each other are still pronounced separately.

- As you will be utilizing the Fidel more in the following sections, we suggest you familiarize yourself with the Fidel Phonic Code. You can refer to Activity 2 on page 18 to help you locate sounds and words n the Fidel and Word Charts.

Table 1.1 Activity 1

Sound / Spelling
- Existing Sounds/spellings: a u i e o
- New Sound/spelling: p as in pat

Materials
- Reading Primers R_0 & R_1
- Pointer
- Fidel

Beginning Notes

Table 1.1 Activity 1

Steps

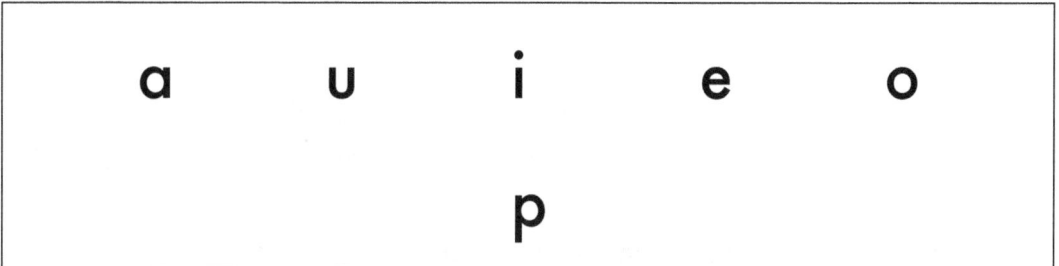

Table 1.1 from Reading Primers R₀ & R₁, Page 28

Making Simple Syllables

- In Table 1.1 of R₁, point to a vowel (for example, <u>a</u>) and ask your student to say it.

- Then sliding your pointer quickly from <u>a</u> to <u>p</u> say: "<u>a</u> followed by this one (<u>p</u>) is called <u>ap</u>."

- Say it only once then point again and let your student say it.

- At this time, it is not helpful and could be distracting to say "<u>ap</u> as in <u>apple</u>."

- Then slide your pointer from each of the other vowels to the <u>p</u> and let your student find out what to say for the resulting syllables. Ask them: "What would you say for this one?"

    - <u>u</u>   followed by <u>p</u> → <u>up</u>
    - <u>i</u>   followed by <u>p</u> → <u>ip</u>
    - <u>e</u>   followed by <u>p</u> → <u>ep</u>
    - <u>o</u>   followed by <u>p</u> → <u>op</u>

- Remember do not name the letters. At this time, just point to the vowel followed by the consonant.

Table 1.1 Activity 1

Teaching Techniques and Games

Oral Dictation:

Teacher writes down, in large size, a number of syllables and "sentences" and says a syllable (<u>ap</u>) or a "sentence" (<u>ap</u> <u>up</u> <u>up</u> <u>op</u>) and your student then:

- option 1: Finds the syllable or sentence and points to it on the paper
- option 2: Taps out the syllable or sentence on the Fidel or R_1
- option 3: Writes the syllable or sentence

Visual Dictation:

Teacher taps out a "syllable" for example, <u>ep</u> or a "sentence" for example, <u>ip</u> <u>apap</u> <u>ep</u>.

- Student says the syllable or "sentence", then
- Student writes the syllable or "sentence"
- Teacher asks "What would the reverse of this be?"
- Teacher asks "Tap it yourself."

Table 1.1 Activity 2

Sound / Spelling
- p as in pat

Materials
- Chart 1
- Reading Primers R_0 & R_1
- Pointer

Beginning Notes

Table 1.1 Activity 2

Steps

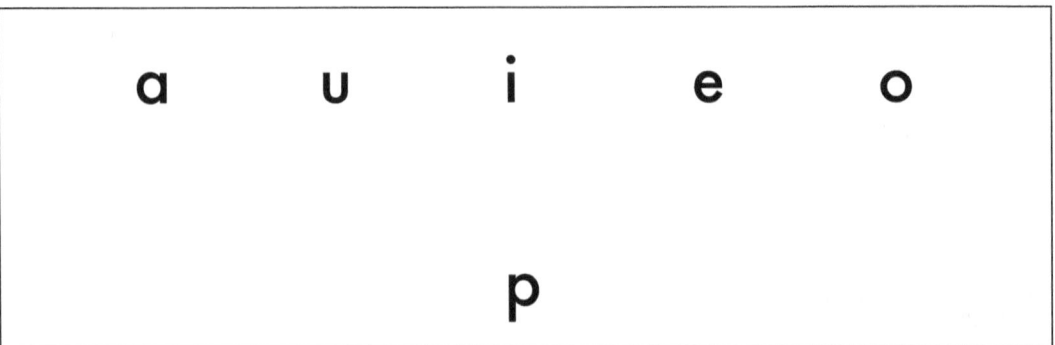

Table 1.1 from Reading Primers R₀ & R₁, Page 28

Reversing Syllables

- Using either Table 1.1 or the Fidel, slide your pointer from p to each of the other vowels and let your student find out what to say for the resulting syllables.

- Ask them: "What would you say for this one?"
    - p followed by a → pa
    - p followed by u → pu
    - p followed by i → pi
    - p followed by e → pe
    - p followed by o → po

- Make sure you give your student enough time to figure out how to sound out the syllables by themselves.

- If you are having difficulties, go back to Table 1.1 Activity 1 on page 39.

Table 1.1 Activity 2

Teaching Techniques and Games

Oral Dictation:

Teacher writes down, in large size, a number of syllables and "sentences" and says a syllable for example, pa or a "sentence" for example, pa pu pi pe and your student then:

- option 1: Finds the syllable or sentence and points to it
- option 2: Taps out the syllable or sentence
- option 3: Writes the syllable or sentence

Visual Dictation:

Teacher taps out a syllable for example, pe or a "sentence" for example, pi pepapi pepu.

- Student says the syllable or "sentence," then
- Student writes the syllable or "sentence"
- Teacher asks "What would the reverse of this be?"
- Teacher asks "Tap it yourself."

Table 1.1 Activity 3

Sound / Spelling
- p as in the word pat

Materials
- Chart 1
- Reading Primers R_0 & R_1
- Pointer

Beginning Notes

Table 1.1 Activity 3

Steps

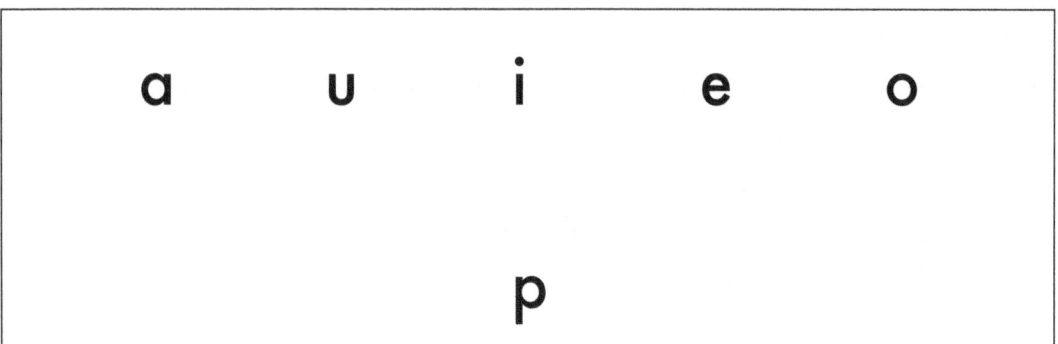

Table 1.1 from Reading Primers R₀ & R₁, Page 28

Combining Syllables to Form Simple Words

- Slide your pointer from the p to the a and then back to the p so that you have tapped out the "word" pap. Then let your student find out how you would pronounce this.

- Go slow and give a lot of time if needed. If they struggle with this have them say pa and then ap. to see if they can make the connection. If they continue to struggle, it is suggested you try the teaching technique on page 111.

- Ask them: "What would you say for this one?"

  - p followed by a followed by p → pap
  - p followed by u followed by p → pup
  - p followed by i followed by p → pip
  - p followed by e followed by p → pep
  - p followed by o followed by p → pop

- Make sure you give your student enough time to figure out how to sound out the syllables by themself.

Table 1.1 Activity 3

Teaching Techniques and Games

Oral Dictation:

- Teacher writes down, in large size, a number of words and "sentences" and says a word:
  - option 1: Student finds the word points to it,
  - option 2: Student taps out the word
  - option 3: Student writes the word

Visual Dictation:

- Teacher taps out a word
  - Student says the syllable or "sentence", then
  - Student writes the syllable or "sentence"
  - Teacher asks "What would the reverse of this be?"
  - Teacher asks "Tap it yourself."

Substitution Game

- Teacher writes a word; pop and asks the student to read it. Then they write a second word; pap and asks the student read it. Next the teacher asks the student which letter do I have to change if I want to transform the pop into the word pap. Continue this game with other words:

  - pip → pep
  - pep → pap
  - pep → pup
  - pop → pep
  - pip → pop, etc.

Table 1.1 Activity 4

Sound / Spelling
- p as in the word pat

Materials
- Reading Primers R_0 & R_1
- Pointer
- Fidel

Beginning Notes
Make sure you give your student enough time to figure out how to sound out the sentence by themselves. It is very important to give as much time as needed and not give the answers when your student encounters some difficulty. If it is too challenging, go back to the previous step and build up from there. All the achievements gained here will result in acceleration in subsequent studies if you do not give answers and give the time needed to figure out what is required.

Table 1.1 Activity 4

Steps

Table 1.1 from Reading Primers R₀ & R₁, Page 28

Combining Words to Form Simple Sentences

- You are now going to use your pointer and either Table 1.1 or the Fidel to tap out the simple sentence:
  pop up.

- First, tap the sequence p o p

- Next you will need to indicate the space or pause between the word pop and up. To do this, use the pointer to tap in a neutral location, such as off the page or on the desk.

- Then tap the sequence u p.

- You will need to explain to your student that when you tap in the neutral location it indicates a new word. Practice this a few times until it is well understood. Then, tap out the following sentences and ask your student: "What would you say for…"

  - pop up
  - pep up
  - up up up
  - up pop up
  - pep up pop

Table 1.1 Activity 4

Teaching Techniques and Games

Oral Dictation Game
Extend the game you learned in Table 1.1 Activity 3 by:

- Tapping out a word or sentence and after it has been successfully spoken, tap it out again and add on to it. The game continues as long as each sequence is spoken correctly

- Tapping out a word or sentence and saying it first in the usual way and then saying it in unusual ways by putting stress – loud or soft – on various parts of the sequence.

Visual Dictation Game
Extend the game you learned in Table 1.1 Activity 3 by: saying sentences with different tones and expression:

- like you are asking a question
- like you are angry
- like you are happy
- like you are confused
- create your own unique ways of expression

Substitution Game
- "What word do you have to change to transform the first sentence into the second?" "pop up" → "pep up"

- Continue this game and create your own sentences.

Reversing Game
- "What does a word like pip become when reversed?"

- "What does a sentence like "up pop" become when reversed?" (Answer is "pop up")

- Continue this game with your own words and sentences.

Table 1.2 Activity 1

Sound / Spelling
- <u>t</u> as in the word te<u>st</u>

Materials
- Reading Primers R_0 & R_1
- Pointer
- Fidel

Beginning Notes
Make sure you give your student enough time to figure out how to sound out the sentence by himself or herself.

It is very important to give as much time as is needed and not to give the answers when your student encounters some difficulty. If it is too challenging, go back to the previous step and build up from there. All the achievements gained here will result in acceleration in subsequent studies if you do not give answers and give the time needed to figure out what is required.

Table 1.2 has a similar structure to Table 1.1. We are introducing the spelling <u>t</u>.

Table 1.2 Activity 1

Steps

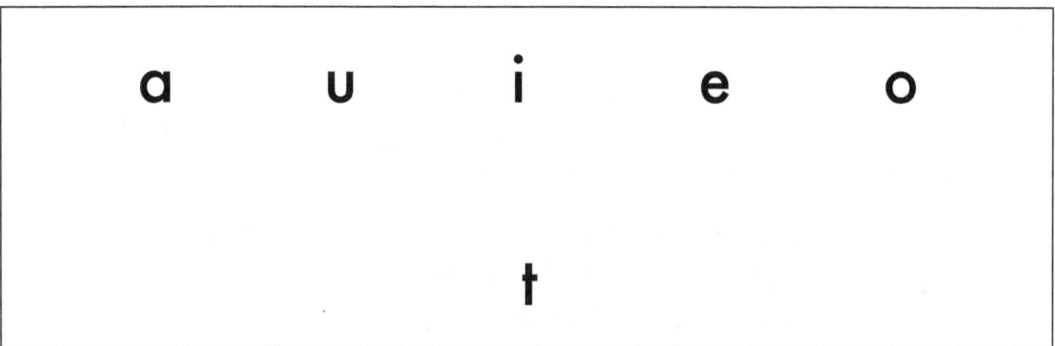

Table 1.2 from Reading Primers R$_0$ & R$_1$, Page 30

Making Simple Syllables

- Using Table 1.1 or the Fidel point to a vowel (for example, <u>a</u>) and ask your student to say it.

- Then sliding your pointer quickly from <u>a</u> to <u>t</u> say: "<u>a</u> followed by this one (<u>t</u>) is called <u>at</u>."

- Say it only once then point again and let your student say it.

- Then slide your pointer from each of the other vowels to the <u>t</u> and let your student find out what to say for the resulting syllables. Ask them: "What would you say for this one?"

    - <u>u</u>   followed by   <u>t</u>   →   <u>ut</u>
    - <u>i</u>   followed by   <u>t</u>   →   <u>it</u>
    - <u>e</u>   followed by   <u>t</u>   →   <u>et</u>
    - <u>o</u>   followed by   <u>t</u>   →   <u>ot</u>

- Remember do not name the letters. At this time, just point to the vowel followed by the consonant.

Table 1.2 Activity 1

Teaching Techniques and Games

Oral Dictation:

Teacher writes down, in large size, a number of syllables and "sentences" and says a syllable for example, <u>at</u> or a "sentence" for example, <u>at</u> <u>ut</u> <u>ut</u> <u>ot</u> and your student then:

- option 1: Finds the syllable or sentence and points to it
- option 2: Taps out the syllable or sentence
- option 3: Writes the syllable or sentence

Visual Dictation:

Teacher taps out a "syllable" for example <u>et</u> or a "sentence" for example, <u>it</u> <u>at</u> <u>et</u>.

- Student says the syllable or "sentence," then
- Student writes the syllable or "sentence"
- Teacher asks "What would the reverse of this be?"
- Teacher asks "Tap it yourself."

Table 1.2 Activity 2

Sound / Spelling
- <u>t</u> as in the word <u>t</u>es<u>t</u>

Materials
- Reading Primers R_0 & R_1
- Pointer
- Fidel

Beginning Notes

Table 1.2 Activity 2

Steps

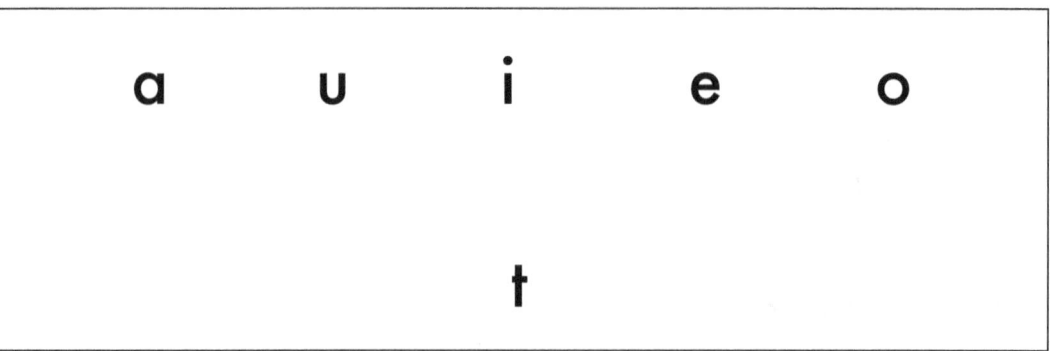

Table 1.2 from Reading Primers R₀ & R₁, Page 30

Reversing Syllables

- Using Table 1.2 or the Fidel, slide your pointer from <u>t</u> to each of the other vowels and let your student find out what to say for the resulting syllables.

- Ask them: "What would you say for this one?"

    - <u>t</u> followed by   <u>a</u> → <u>ta</u>
    - <u>t</u> followed by   <u>u</u> → <u>tu</u>
    - <u>t</u> followed by   <u>i</u> → <u>ti</u>
    - <u>t</u> followed by   <u>e</u> → <u>te</u>
    - <u>t</u> followed by   <u>o</u> → <u>to</u>

- Make sure you give your student enough time to figure out how to sound out the syllables by themself.

Table 1.2 Activity 2

Teaching Techniques and Games

Oral Dictation:

Teacher writes down, in large size, a number of syllables and "sentences" and says a syllable for example, <u>ta</u> or a "sentence" for example, <u>ta</u> <u>tu</u> <u>ti</u> <u>te</u> and your student then:

- option 1: Finds the syllable or sentence and points to it
- option 2: Taps out the syllable or sentence
- option 3: Writes the syllable or sentence

Visual Dictation:

Teacher taps out a "syllable" for example, <u>te</u> or a "sentence" for example, <u>ti</u> <u>tetati</u> <u>tetu</u>.

- Student says the syllable or "sentence," then
- Student writes the syllable or "sentence"
- Teacher asks "What would the reverse of this be?"
- Teacher asks "Tap it yourself."

Table 1.2 Activity 3

Sound / Spelling
- <u>t</u> as in the word <u>t</u>es<u>t</u>

Materials
- Reading Primers R_0 & R_1
- Pointer
- Fidel

Beginning Notes

Table 1.2 Activity 3

Steps

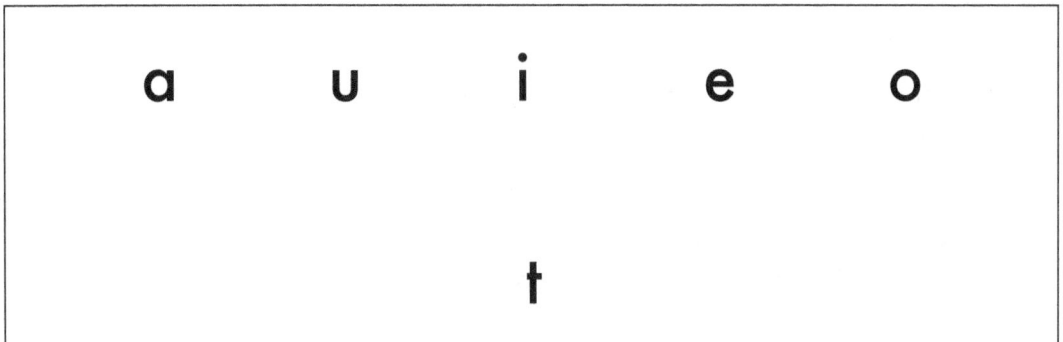

Table 1.2 from Reading Primers R₀ & R₁, Page 30

Combining Syllables to Form Simple Words

- Using Table 1.2 or the Fidel, slide your pointer from the <u>t</u> to the <u>a</u> and then back to the <u>t</u> so that you have tapped out the "word" <u>tat</u>. Then let your student find out how you would pronounce this. Go slow and give a lot of time if needed. If they struggle with this have them say <u>ta</u> and then <u>at</u> to see if they can make the connection.

- Ask them: "What would you say for this one?"

    - <u>t</u> followed by   <u>a</u> followed by <u>t</u> → <u>tat</u>
    - <u>t</u> followed by   <u>u</u> followed by <u>t</u> → <u>tut</u>
    - <u>t</u> followed by   <u>i</u> followed by <u>t</u> → <u>tit</u>
    - <u>t</u> followed by   <u>e</u> followed by <u>t</u> → <u>tet</u>
    - <u>t</u> followed by   <u>o</u> followed by <u>t</u> → <u>tot</u>

- Make sure you give you student enough time to figure out how to sound out the syllables by themselves.

Table 1.2 Activity 3

Teaching Techniques and Games

Oral Dictation:

- Teacher writes down, in large size, a number of words and "sentences" and says a word:
  - option 1: Student finds the word points to it
  - option 2: Student taps out the word
  - option 3: Student writes the word

Visual Dictation:

- Teacher taps out a word
  - Student says the syllable or "sentence", then
  - Student writes the syllable or "sentence"
  - Teacher asks "What would the reverse of this be?"
  - Teacher asks "Tap it yourself."

Substitution Game:

- Teacher writes a word; tot and asks the student to read it. Then they write a second word; tat and asks the student read it. Next the teacher asks the student which letter do I have to change if I want to transform the tot into the word tat. Continue this game with other words:
  - tit → tet
  - tet → tat
  - tet → tut
  - tot → tet
  - tit → tot, etc.

Table 1.2 Activity 4

Sound / Spelling

- <u>t</u> as in the word <u>t</u>es<u>t</u>

Materials

- Chart 1
- Reading Primers R_0 & R_1
- Pointer
- Fidel

Beginning Notes

Make sure you give your student enough time to figure out how to sound out the sentence by himself or herself.

It is very important to give as much time as is needed and not to give the answers when your student encounters some difficulty. If it is too challenging, go back to the previous step and build up from there. All the achievements gained here will result in acceleration in subsequent studies if you do not give answers and give the time needed to figure out what is required.

Table 1.2 Activity 4

Steps

Table 1.2 from Reading Primers R₀ & R₁, Page 30

Combining Words to Form Simple Sentences

- Using Table 1.2 or the Fidel, you are now going to use your pointer to tap out the simple sentence:
  <u>at</u> <u>it</u>.

- First, tap the sequence <u>a</u> <u>t</u>

- Next you will need to indicate the space or pause between the word <u>at</u> and <u>it</u>. To do this, use the pointer to tap in a neutral location, such as off the bottom of the page.

- Then tap the sequence <u>i</u> <u>t</u>.

- You will need to explain to your student that when you tap in the neutral location it indicates a new word. Practice this a few times until it is well understood. Then, tap out the following sentences and ask your student: "What would you say for…"

    - <u>at</u> <u>it</u>
    - <u>tot</u> <u>it</u> <u>up</u>
    - <u>tit</u> <u>tat</u>
    - <u>tat</u> <u>it</u>
    - <u>tut</u> <u>tut</u> <u>tut</u>

Table 1.2 Activity 4

Teaching Techniques and Games

Oral Dictation Game

Extend this game by:

- tapping out a word or sentence and after it has been successfully spoken, tap it out again and add on to it. The game continues as long as each sequence is spoken correctly
- tapping out a word or sentence and saying it first in the usual way and then saying it in unusual ways by putting stress – loud or soft – on various parts of the sequence.

Visual Dictation Game

Extend this game by saying sentences in with different tones and expression:

- like you are asking a question
- like you are angry
- like you are happy
- like you are confused
- like you are singing
- create your own unique ways of expression

Reversing Game

- "What does a word like <u>tat</u> become when reversed?"
- "What does a sentence like "<u>tit tat</u>" become when reversed?" (Answer is: "<u>tat tit</u>")
- Continue this game with your own words and sentences.

Practice Using Chart 1

- Now that we have covered p and t, play the Oral Dictation Game using Chart 1: pat, pit, pet, pot, pop, at, it, up, tot, top, tip, tap, apt
- At this point, we have left out putt, we will discuss this in Table 1.3

Table 1.3 Activity 1

Sound / Spelling
- pp as in the word puppet
- tt as in the word putt

Materials
- Chart 1
- Reading Primers R_0 & R_1
- Pointer
- Fidel

Beginning Notes

In this Table, we introduce our first ambiguity. We will show that a different spelling can have a similar sound. We will introduce the student to the spelling pp and tt

Notice that the pp and tt are located in the same column as p and t on the Fidel. This indicates they have the same sound. Ask the student "What do you notice about the spellings pp and tt?" They might say that they have the same color or they are in the same column as the letter p and t respectively.

Make sure you give your student enough time to figure out how to sound out the sentence by himself or herself.

It is very important to give as much time as needed and not give the answers when your student encounters some difficulty. If it is too challenging, go back to the previous step and build up from there. All the achievements gained here will result in acceleration in subsequent studies if you do not give answers and give the time needed to figure out what is required.

Table 1.3 Activity 1

Steps

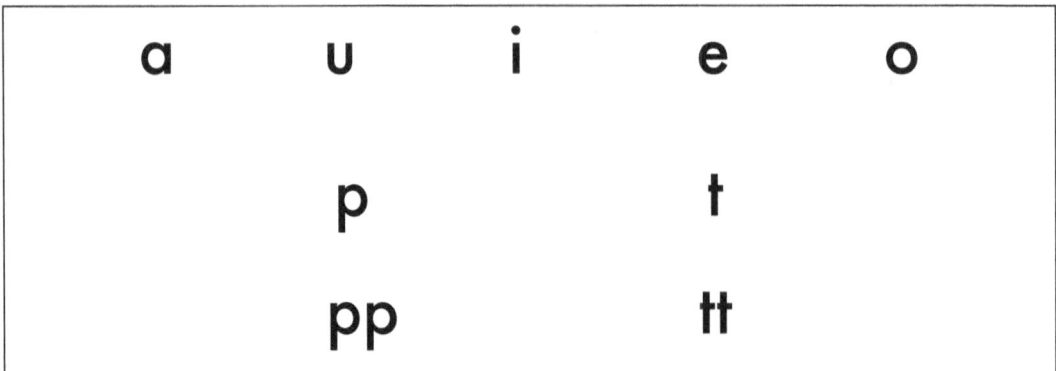

Table 1.3 from Reading Primers R₀ & R₁, Page 32

Note: Depending on the pace of your student, you may break the steps below into multiple lessons.

Making Simple Syllables and Forming Simple Words

Tap out various spelling and ask the student to say the words

- p followed by   u   followed by tt   →   putt
- p followed by   i   followed by tt   →   pitt
- p followed by   o   followed by tt   →   pott
- t followed by   o   followed by pp   →   topp

Break the above into 3 steps if the student is having trouble. i.e. p followed by u; then u followed by tt; then combine to form putt.

Combining Words to Form Simple Sentences

Use the techniques described in Activities for previous Tables to form the sentences found in the section under Table 1.3 in R₁:

- tap it
- pitt tip it up
- tip it up pitt
- putt it, etc.

Table 1.3 Activity 1

Teaching Techniques and Games

At this stage, you should be familiar with the games and exercises we have introduced in the previous lessons. We have summarized them in the Toolbox of Games, Exercises & Teaching Techniques found on page 93. It is suggested you incorporate some of the following techniques to add variety, and increase interest for your student:

- Oral Dictation
- Visual Dictation
- Substitution Game
- Reversing Game

Practice these games using Chart 1. Add the word <u>putt</u> found on the second line in Chart 1 to the game played in Table 1.2 Activity 4. Tap out different sentences using Chart 1 by building on the knowledge gained in previous lessons.

Table 1.4 Activity 1

Sound / Spelling
- <u>s</u> as in <u>is</u>

Materials
- Chart 1
- Reading Primers R$_0$ & R$_1$
- Pointer
- Fidel

Beginning Notes

In this Table, we introduce another ambiguity with <u>s</u>. The letter <u>s</u> can have multiple sounds. For example, the letter <u>s</u> in the word <u>is</u> sounds differently than the word <u>us</u>. In this section, we are introducing the "lilac" <u>s</u> as in <u>is</u>. This is the 3rd column on the bottom half of the Fidel. Later, in Table 1.6, we will introduce the "lime green" <u>s</u> as in <u>us</u>.

Make sure you give your student enough time to figure out how to sound out the sentence by himself or herself.

It is very important to give as much time as is needed and not to give the answers when your student encounters some difficulty. If it is too challenging, go back to the previous step and build up from there. All the achievements gained here will result in acceleration in subsequent studies if you do not give answers and give the time needed to figure out what is required.

Table 1.4 Activity 1

Steps

a	u	i	e		o
		s			

Table 1.4 from Reading Primers R₀ & R₁, Page 36

Note: Depending on the pace of your student, you may break the below into multiple lessons.

Making Simple Syllables and Forming Simple Words

- Tap out various spellings and ask the student to say the words
    - a followed by   s → as
    - u followed by   s → us (remember to pronounce it like uz)
    - i followed by   s → is
    - e followed by   s → es
    - o followed by   s → os

Combining Words to Form Simple Sentences

- Use the techniques described in Activities for previous Tables to form the sentences found in the section under Table 1.4 in R₁:
    - as is, etc.

Table 1.4 Activity 1

Teaching Techniques and Games

At this stage, you should be familiar with the games and exercises we have introduced in the previous lessons. We have summarized them in the Toolbox of Games, Exercises & Teaching Techniques found on page 93. It is suggested you incorporate some of the following techniques to add variety, and increase interest for your student:

- Oral Dictation
- Visual Dictation
- Substitution Game
- Reversing Game
- Practice Using Chart 1

Add the words <u>as</u> and <u>is</u> found on the fourth line in Chart 1 to the game played in Table 1.2 Activity 4. Tap out different sentences using Chart 1 by building on the knowledge gained in previous lessons

As a note, you may have noticed <u>-s</u> on Word Chart 1. This represents a plural form of the word. This will be discussed in Table 1.6.

Table 1.5 Activity 1

Sound / Spelling
- No new sounds/spelling

Materials
- Chart 1
- Reading Primers R_0 & R_1
- Pointer
- Fidel

Beginning Notes

In this Table, we practice the spellings we have already covered to build more complex sentences.

Make sure you give your student enough time to figure out how to sound out the sentence by himself or herself.

It is very important to give as much time as is needed and not to give the answers when your student encounters some difficulty. If it is too challenging, go back to the previous step and build up from there. All the achievements gained here will result in acceleration in subsequent studies if you do not give answers and give the time needed to figure out what is required.

Table 1.5 Activity 1

Steps

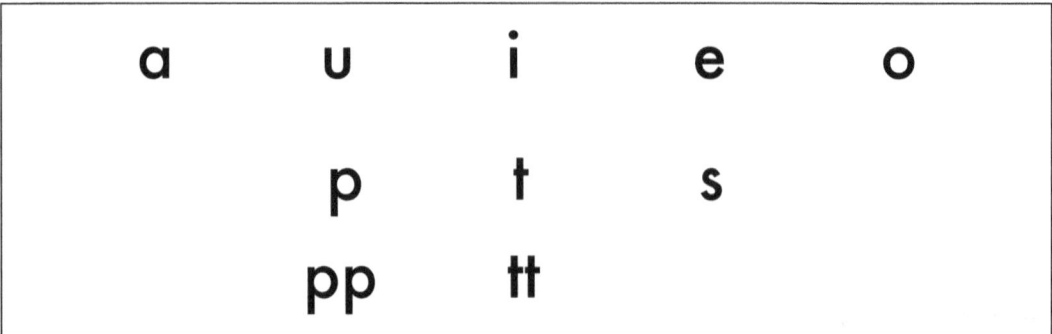

Table 1.5 from Reading Primers R₀ & R₁, Page 38

- Depending on the pace of your student, you may break the below into multiple lessons.
    - Making simple syllables and combining syllables to form simple words
    - Combining words to form simple sentences
- Use the techniques described in Activities for previous Tables to form the sentences found in the section under Table 1.5 in R₁:
    - is it
    - is it pop
    - is pop up
    - pat is as apt as pitt is , etc.

Table 1.5 Activity 1

Teaching Techniques and Games

At this stage, you should be familiar with the games and exercises we have introduced in the previous lessons. We have summarized them in the Toolbox of Games, Exercises & Teaching Techniques found on page 93. It is suggested you incorporate some of the following techniques to add variety, and increase interest for your student:

- Oral Dictation
- Visual Dictation
- Substitution Game
- Reversing Game
- Practice Using Chart 1

Tap out different sentences using Chart 1 by building on the knowledge gained in previous lessons

As a note, you may have noticed -s on Word Chart 1. This represents a plural form of the word. This will be discussed in Table 1.6.

Table 1.6 Activity 1

Sound / Spelling
- s as in us
- 's as in tom's
- ss as in asset

Materials
- Chart 1
- Reading Primers R_0 & R_1
- Pointer
- Fidel

Beginning Notes

In this Table, we introduce another ambiguity with s. The letter s can have multiple sounds. For example, the letter s in the word is sounds differently than the word us. In this section, we are introducing the "lime green" s as in us. This is the 4th column on the bottom half of the Fidel. previously, in Table 1.4, we introduced the "lilac" s as in is.

Make sure you give your student enough time to figure out how to sound out the sentence by himself or herself.

It is very important to give as much time as is needed and not to give the answers when your student encounters some difficulty. If it is too challenging, go back to the previous step and build up from there. All the achievements gained here will result in acceleration in subsequent studies if you do not give answers and give the time needed to figure out what is required.

Table 1.6 Activity 1

Steps

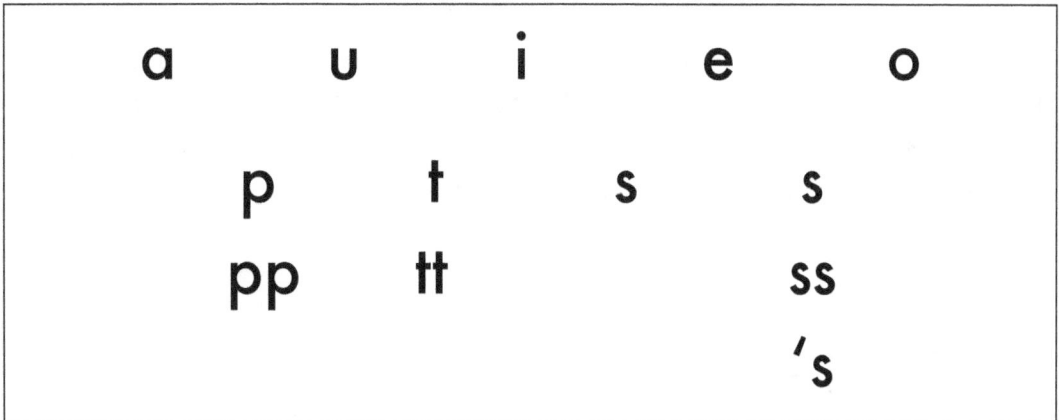

Table 1.6 from Reading Primers R₀ & R₁, Page 40

Note: Depending on the pace of your student, you may break the below into multiple lessons.

- Making simple syllables and combining syllables to form simple words

  - <u>as</u>
  - <u>us</u>   (here, pronounce it as you would the word us)
  - <u>is</u>   (here, pronounce it as you would the word this), etc.

- Introduce the possessive form of nouns and contractions

  - Possessive: <u>pat's</u>, <u>pitt's</u>
  - Contractions: <u>it's</u>, <u>it's pitt</u>, <u>it's pop</u>

- Combining words to form simple sentences

- Use the techniques described in Activities for previous Tables to form the sentences found in the section under Table 1.6 in R₁

Table 1.6 Activity 1

Teaching Techniques and Games

At this stage, you should be familiar with the games and exercises we have introduced in the previous lessons. We have summarized them in the Toolbox of Games, Exercises & Teaching Techniques found on page 93. It is suggested you incorporate some of the following techniques to add variety, and increase interest for your student:

- Oral Dictation
- Visual Dictation
- Substitution Game
- Reversing Game
- Practice Using Chart 1

Tap out different sentences using Chart 1 by building on the knowledge gained in previous lessons

We have not covered the letter e in the word puppet on Word Chart 1. As you may have noticed the color of e is the same as i, thus pronounced the same. Ask your student to try to pronounce this word. He or she may be able to get it immediately. Do not be tempted to give the answer, but instead provide leading questions such as:

- "What do you notice about this letter?"

If they are still stuck, you can ask them:

- "What color is the e? Does it look like any other color we have covered?"

The Word Building Tables

Congratulations on completing the first part of R₁. At this stage, we have shown you the 1st Word Building Table. Your student can now construct basic words and sentences in the English language.

The Word Building Tables reflect the novelty of Words in Color. They contain no words. Instead, each table presents a set of signs corresponding to a given set of sounds. By glancing at the successive tables, one can understand the organization of the Fidel. Table 1.6 in R₁, for instance, tells us that the printed signs correspond to seven different sounds: 5 vowel sounds a, u, i, e, o and 4 consonant sounds.

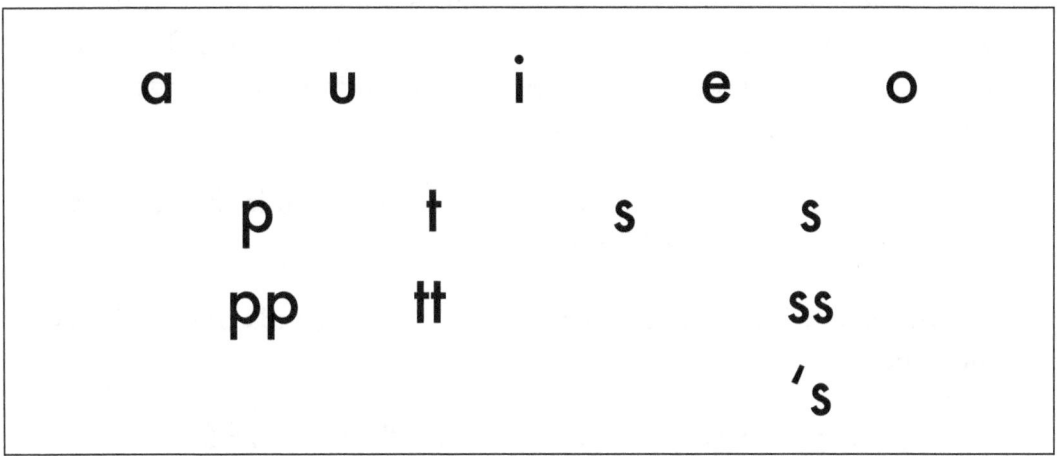

Table 1.6 from Reading Primers R₀ & R₁, Page 40

That t and tt are in the same column indicates that they are different spellings for the same sound (as in pat and putt for example). This organization is maintained throughout the tables. Each successive table introduces both (1) new sounds which appear in new columns and (2) new spellings for the sounds already met.

The Word Building Tables

The pointing and sliding techniques mentioned when introducing the consonants can be used with the Word Building Table. You can let your student take the pointer and ask him or her to make up as many words as he or she can using Table 1.6. Then ask the student to compare their list to those words contained in Reading Primer R_1, and Word Chart 1. Did he or she find some words that were not on the chart or in the book?

The Word Building Tables are a tool with a number of useful characteristics:

- They present a sequence of restricted signs. Therefore, any student can master the techniques of generating words while still working with very few sounds and very few complicated spellings. This same technique of making words will be used when the student has been introduced to all of the sounds and spellings of English.

- It offers your student tools to generate words found in the reading primers or on the Word Charts.

- It gives him or her a progressive record of the sounds and spellings they know.

- Once your student becomes acquainted with the Word Building Tables' special features, they will be ready to use the tables in their work.

Introducing The Gap Game

This game is played to develop insight into word formation. The teacher could start with an example of how to play the game by saying:

- "Lets look at the word pat."
- "If we replace p by a gap it will look like _ a t and three words can come to mind: pat, sat, tat."
- "If we replace a by a gap we get p _ t and four words come to mind pat, pit, pet, pot using the known vowels."
- "If we replace t by a gap we get pa _ which brings to mind pap and pass as well as pat."
- "Now lets play this game with the following words..."

As long as this game is interesting to all, you can play this game for hours just starting with any word already met and creating a gap for which perhaps there is more than one answer.

For example: stop, can call for four places for a gap: _ top, s _ op, st _ p, and sto _ only the third providing alternative words when using the vowels known: stop and step. The word stock or store will not come to mind at the stage we are at now.

The Gap Game Demonstrates:

- That signs can be taken out of words, from any place, and the words can still be developed by the learners;

- That the student's image of words is flexible enough so that an incomplete pattern can bring to him or her a number of answers;

- That the same word can provide answers to a number of differently formulated questions;

- That not all questions have the same number of answers. There is no obligation to start with the first column; any example can be a starting point.

Word Building Table 2

On Page 45 of Reading Primers R₀ & R₁ you will find Word Building Table 2.

a	u	i	e	o	a	y	I
		o	e				
p	t	s	s	m	n		y
pp	tt		ss	mm	nn		
		's	's	'm			

Word Building Table 2.0 from Reading Primers R₀ & R₁, Page 45

This table is made of the five vowels studied in R₀ the four consonant sounds, with eight different spellings that were introduced in Tables 1.1-1.6 and adds:

The vowels:
- a as in the article a
- o as in son
- y as in puppy
- I as in the first person I

The consonants:
- m as in man
- mm as in mommy
- n as in pant
- nn as in penny
- 'm as in I'm
- y as in yes

Word Building Table 2

Notes Before you Begin:

By the end of the next two Tables, you will have completed R_1.

We suggest you practice using the same discipline as you did in previous sections to ensure the student clearly grasps the sound, spelling and concepts.

On Chart 2 there are two signs that some beginners tend to confuse and which we do not introduce by name, but by color: the "orange" three-legged m and the "lavender" two-legged n. Thus, we have broken these two spellings into two lessons

Table 2.1 Activity 1

Sound / Spelling

The consonants:
- m as in man
- 'm as in I'm

The vowels:
- a as in the article a
- I as in the first person I

Materials

- Chart 2
- Reading Primers R_0 & R_1
- Pointer
- Fidel

Beginning Notes

Make sure you give your student enough time to figure out how to sound out the sentence by himself or herself.

It is very important to give as much time as is needed and not to give the answers when your student encounters some difficulty. If it is too challenging, go back to the previous step and build up from there. All the achievements gained here will result in acceleration in subsequent studies if you do not give answers and give the time needed to figure out what is required.

There are more examples of words using the new sounds and spellings than there are in this guide. Consult the Reference Guide to the Fidel Phonic Code for more examples.

Table 2.1 Activity 1

Steps

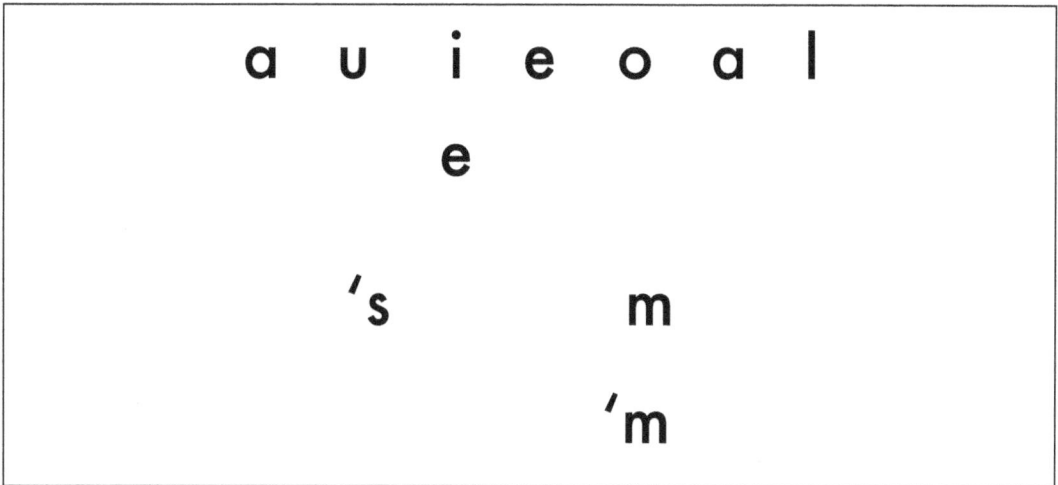

Table 2.1 from Reading Primers R₀ & R₁, Page 46

Note: Depending on the pace of your student, you may break the below into multiple lessons.

Making Simple Syllables and Forming Simple Words

- Tap out various spellings and ask the student to say the words
    - <u>a</u> followed by   <u>tt e m p t</u>   →   <u>a</u>ttempt
    - <u>m</u> followed by   <u>a t</u>   →   <u>m</u>at
    - <u>p</u> followed by   <u>u m p</u>   →   <u>p</u>ump
    - etc.

Combining Words to Form Simple Sentences

- Use the techniques described in Activities for previous Tables to form the sentences found in the section under Table 2.1 in R_1:

  - <u>it</u> <u>is</u> <u>mom's</u>

  - <u>I</u> <u>miss</u> <u>pop</u>

  - etc.

Table 2.1 Activity 1

Teaching Techniques and Games

At this stage, you should be familiar with the games and exercises we have introduced in the previous lessons. We have summarized them in the Toolbox of Games, Exercises & Teaching Techniques found on page 93. It is suggested you incorporate some of the following techniques to add variety, and increase interest for your student:

- Oral Dictation
- Visual Dictation
- Substitution Game
- Reversing Game

Practice Using Chart 2

- Use various games to practice Chart 2
- Build upon previous knowledge to pronounce the words on this chart. By this stage the student will be able to pronounce words such as:

    - mat tim met tom mom must mumps mast I mops miss mess pump am stamps map sum I'm and pam

Table 2.2 Activity 1

Sound / Spelling

The consonants:
- mm as in mommy
- n as in pant
- nn as in penny
- y as in yes

The vowels:
- o as in son
- y as in puppy

Materials
- Chart 2
- Reading Primers R_0 & R_1
- Pointer
- Fidel

Beginning Notes

Make sure you give you student enough time to figure out how to sound out the sentence by himself or herself.

It is very important to give as much time as is needed and not to give the answers when your student encounters some difficulty. If it is too challenging, go back to the previous step and build up from there. All the achievements gained here will result in acceleration in subsequent studies if you do not give answers and give the time need to figure out what is required.

Table 2.2 Activity 1

Steps

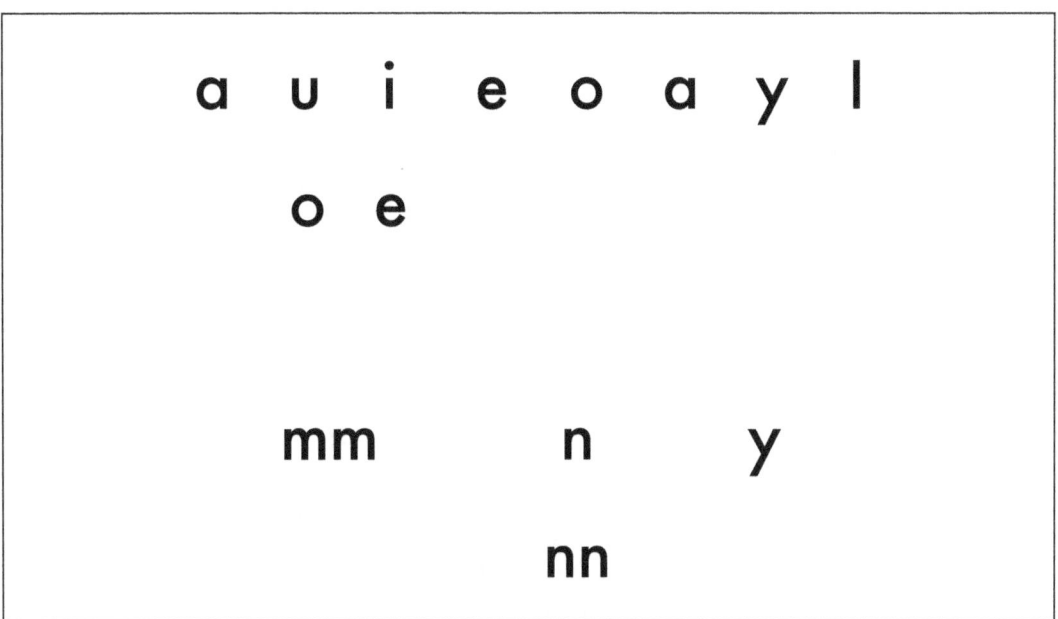

Table 2.2 from Reading Primers R₀ & R₁, Page 50

Making Simple Syllables and Forming Simple Words

- Tap out various spelling and ask the student to say the words
  - <u>o</u> followed by   <u>n</u>   →   <u>on</u>
  - <u>y</u> followed by   <u>u mm y</u>   →   <u>yummy</u>
    (this example gives two sounds of the spelling <u>y</u>)
  - etc.

Combining Words to Form Simple Sentences

- Use the techniques described in Activities for previous Tables to form the sentences found in the section under Table 2.2 in R_1:

    - <u>sam</u> is <u>a</u> <u>man</u>
    - <u>I</u> <u>miss</u> <u>pop</u>
    - etc.

Table 2.2 Activity 1

Teaching Techniques and Games

At this stage, you should be familiar with the games and exercises we have introduced in the previous lessons. We have summarized them in the Toolbox of Games, Exercises & Teaching Techniques found on page 93. It is suggested you to incorporate some of the following techniques to add variety, and increase interest for your student:

- Oral Dictation
- Visual Dictation
- Substitution Game
- Reversing Game
- Practice Using Chart 2

Use various games to practice Chart 2

- Build upon previous knowledge to pronounce the words on this chart. By this stage the student will be able to pronounce words such as:

- not nut net ten man men tent spent sent pants pin sun an in on son tempt attempt assistant

Practice Using Chart 1 & 2

- Build on this challenge by constructing a sentence using the words learned in Charts 1 and 2

Practice Using the Fidel

- For an even more challenging exercise, spell out the words in a sentence using the Fidel. Tap out each spelling separately to make a sentence such as:
  - p a t (blank) i s (blank) a (blank) m a n
- The student should then say: pat is a man

Introducing The Transformation Game

This game creates a new word from a given word. It is one that children and adults enjoy very much after they have become familiar with the rules. It is surprising how involved people get when presented with the challenge of this game. The object of the game is to go from one word to another through a succession of changes, using only four operations, and making only one change at a time:

- (s) substitution (of one sound for another)
- (a) addition (of one sound at the beginning or end of a word)
- (i) insertion (of one sound within a word)
- (r) reversal (of the sounds of a word)

The basis for the game is not single letters but signs, each of which may contain several letters representing one sound. Each step must produce a legitimate English word. In most cases, there is more than one way to go from one word to another.

(Note that subtraction is not permissible in the game, although it is obvious that it can be used for word formation. It would reduce the interest of the game by making almost all challenges much too easy.)

Transformation Game Examples:

Example 1: from <u>at</u> to <u>sips</u>

$$at \xrightarrow{s} it \xrightarrow{a} pit \xrightarrow{r} tip \xrightarrow{a} tips \xrightarrow{s} sips$$

$$at \xrightarrow{a} pat \xrightarrow{r} tap \xrightarrow{s} tip \xrightarrow{s} sip \xrightarrow{a} sips$$

Example 2: from up to tests

```
            s       s      r      s      e      s
         sup  →  sip  →  tip  →  pit  →  pet  →  pest  →  pests
       ↗ s                                                      ↘ s
  up                                                                    tests
       ↘ s                                                      ↗ s
         ups  →  sups  →  sips  →  sits  →  sets  →  pets  →  pests
            u       s      s      s      s      e
```

These exercises correspond to what we did as babies when we first learned to speak. It truly reflects the functionings of the mind. You can easily recognize this when listening to young children play with sounds — they make many words from just a few sounds, then they learn to create different words by changing the order of sounds and adding new ones. These exercises are some of the most effective techniques available to support the development of reading skills from basic to advanced.

The game of transformations enhances this awareness and prepares students to retain the written form of words.

Give your student pairs of words for the game of transformation. Increase the difficulty and complexity of the challenges as the game develops.

You can introduce transformations after your student has completed the study of Reading Primers R_0 & R_1. The exercise can be worked out orally or in writing. Starting with pat, ask him: "How would this word sound with the "ice blue" one instead of the "buff" one?" (pet). Then ask him what other changes he can make (one at a time) to arrive at pits.

In the beginning don't insist on getting results, but rather make sure that the rules are clear and that your student understands what they are supposed to do. The transformation game is played throughout the Words in Color program. You can go back to it and present new challenges whenever you see that your student needs this type of exercise or wants to play the game.

Congratulations On Completing R_1

You have now introduced several consonant sounds.

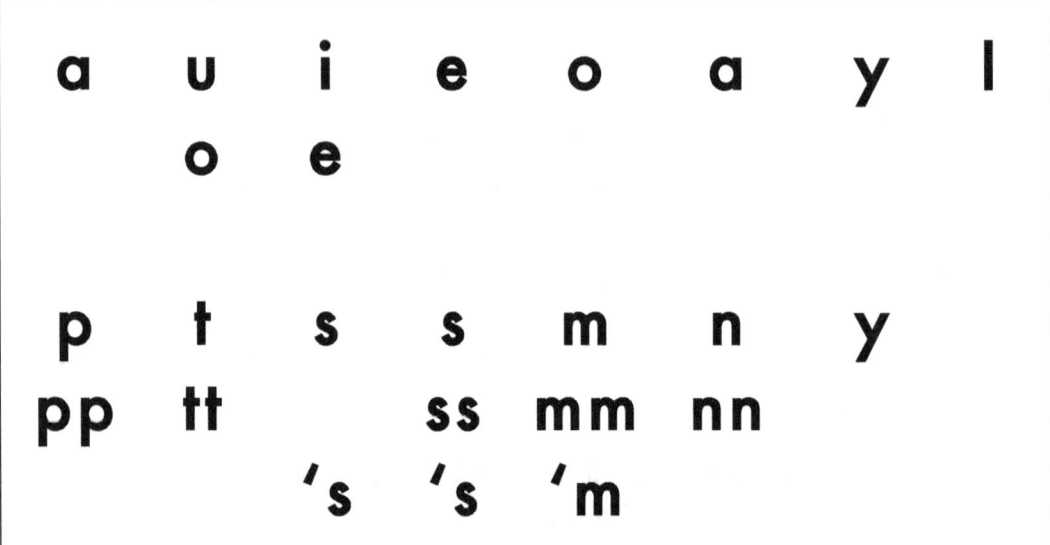

Word Building Table 2 from Reading Primers R_0 & R_1, Page 45

Your student can now begin working on Worksheet 1 found in Workbook 1. If your student is able to pass through the exercises with ease, they can move on to Worksheet 2.

If they are having difficulties with it, it may be beneficial to review some of the previous lessons. By having a solid footing in the concepts introduced above, your student will be able to more easily master the work ahead.

Before you progress to R_2, it is suggested that the student feel comfortable in combining the various sounds and spellings introduced.

R_2, R_3 and Beyond

R_2, R_3 and Beyond

Now that we have shown you the basics to getting started and introduced basic words and sentences, you are now ready to progress to R_2.

Moving forward, we suggest you introduce each sound one at a time using the following techniques:

- Find the sound on the Fidel. If you are having difficulty finding it on the Fidel, use the Color Key for the American English Fidel.

- Tap out the new sound. Remember, you can introduce vowel sounds in isolation, but you must introduce consonants with vowels. For example, to introduce f as in if, tap out i then f for example

- Next, play around with the new sound by combining it with sounds the student already knows. For example, f with a as in at, f with a as in was, etc. At this point it is not important for the words to be real English words as long as the student is correctly identifying the spelling with the correct sound.

- Practice by finding words on the Word Charts that include the new spelling.

- Then, practice by reading the words, sentences in the Student's Reading Primer Books R_0 & R_1, R_2, R_3), then use the Worksheets in Workbooks 1 & 2.

For further resources on how to use and apply Words in Color, please visit the Words in Color section of www.EducationalSolutions.com or visit our blog at www.Re-inventEd.com

Toolbox of Teaching Techniques and Games

Technique: Visual Dictation

Visual Dictation 1

This game is played with the Fidel, and a pointer

- The teacher taps out a sequence of signs, for example: p a t
- When the teacher has finished tapping out the sequence the student says the word: pat

The rhythm and speed of tapping can be varied to make the game more challenging and more interesting.

The complexity and difficulty can be increased or decreased by varying the length of the sequences tapped. For example

- p a → p a t → p a t s

Depth of understanding can be assessed by varying the sequence of signs tapped. For example:

- p a t s → p a s t → s p a t → s p a t s → t a p s

When a student has read the word successfully, the teacher may ask them:

- To tap the word on the Fidel themselves.
- To close their eyes and take a mental photograph of the whole word. This helps with retention.
- To close their eyes and tap the same sequence in the their mind – the teacher could ask them: can you see the first sign, the second, the third and so on. This helps with retention.
- To close their eyes, tap the sequence forward and say the word out loud, then ask what is the reverse of this – say the word, then tap it out. After they have done this with their eyes closed, the teacher could ask them to do it again on the charts. This helps with achieving high levels of performance and retention.

- Say the word with different tones of expression. For example: with happiness, with anger, with confusion, with skepticism, etc. This helps with understanding meaning.

The teacher may also ask one student to assume the role of teacher. In this scenario, one student taps out the sequence, another student reads aloud what has been tapped out.

The teacher could then ask another student, or the whole class; "What do you think? Is it correct?" If they feel it is not correct, the teacher could ask them tap the correct sequence themselves. There are several ways the question can be asked:

- "Is it correct?"
- "What do you think?"
- "Are you 100% sure?"
- "How would change it?"

Visual Dictation 2

Visual dictation 2 has one difference from Visual Dictation 1 – it uses words from the word charts and not the Fidel. For example:

- Using word chart 1, the teacher would tap: <u>pat</u> <u>is</u> <u>top</u>.
- Following this, the student would read aloud the sequence of words tapped.
- If the student has difficulty with one word, the teacher can help them to work through it by using the Fidel and Visual Dictation 1.
- Once the student has worked through the difficult word, then the teacher would re-tap: <u>pat</u> <u>is</u> <u>top</u>.
- Following this, the student would read aloud the sequence of words.

All other techniques applicable for Visual Dictation 1 would apply to Visual Dictation 2.

Technique: Oral Dictation

Oral Dictation 1

This game is played with the Fidel, and a pointer.

- The teacher says a word for example: <u>pat</u>
- The student would then tap out the sequence of signs corresponding to the word: <u>p</u> <u>a</u> <u>t</u>.

The rhythm and speed of the spoken word can be varied to make the game more challenging and more interesting. The complexity and difficulty can be increased or decreased by varying the length of the words or syllables spoken. For example

- <u>pa</u> → <u>pat</u> → <u>pats</u>

Depth of understanding can be assessed by using words that have very similar sounds, but small differences in spelling the sequence of signs tapped. For example, the teacher might say two words and then ask the student to tap them out on the Fidel:

- <u>pats</u> → <u>past</u>   or   <u>spat</u> → <u>spots</u>

Next the teacher might ask: "In what ways are these words different?"

When a student has tapped the word successfully, the teacher may ask them:

- To close their eyes and imagine tapping the word on the Fidel themselves. The teacher could ask them: "What's the first sign/color? The second? The third?" And so on. This helps with retention.
- To take a mental photograph of the word. This helps with retention.
- To close their eyes, tap the sequence forward and say it out loud. Then ask: "What is the reverse of this?" "Say the word, then tap it out." After they have done this with their eyes closed, the teacher

could ask them to do it again on the charts. This helps with achieving high levels of performance and retention.

- Which chart the word is on, and then ask them to find it.
- To say the word with different tones of expression. For example: with happiness, with anger, with confusion, with skepticism, etc. This helps with understanding meaning.

The teacher may also ask one student to assume the role of teacher. In this scenario, one student would say the word, another one then taps out the sequence, and yet another student reads aloud what has been tapped out.

The teacher could then ask another student, or the whole class; "What do you think? Is it correct?" If they feel it is not correct, the teacher could ask them tap the correct sequence themselves. There are several ways the question can be asked:

- "Is it correct?"
- "What do you think?"
- "Are you 100% sure?"
- "How would change it?"

Oral Dictation 2

Oral Dictation 2 has one difference from Oral Dictation 1 - it incorporates words from the word charts in addition to the Fidel. For example:

- Using word chart 1, the teacher would say: <u>top it up</u>.
- Following this, the student would say a loud the sequence of words and then proceed to tap them out.
- If the student has difficulty with one word, the teacher can help then work through it by using the Fidel and Oral Dictation 1.
- When the student has worked through the difficult word, then the teacher would say the full sequence again: <u>top it up</u>.
- The student would then proceed to tap out the sequence again.

All other techniques applicable for Oral Dictation 1 would apply to Oral Dictation 2.

Technique: Substitution Game

Teacher writes a word; pop (for example) and asks the student to read it. Then they write a second word; pap and asks the student read it. Next the teacher asks the student which letter do I have to change if I want to transform the first word (pop) into the second word (pap). This game can be continued with other words. For example:

- pip → pep
- pep → pap
- pep → pup
- pop → pep
- pip → pop
- etc.

The game can also be played with short simple sentences which gradually become more complex. For example, the teacher could:

- Write two sentences on the board: pop up → pep up
- Next they would ask: "What word do you have to change to transform the first sentence into the second?"

Technique: Reversing Game

The Reversing Game will help the student work through a mental exercise of trying to spell and read words and sentences that are in reverse order. For example, the teacher could write a word or sentence on the board, and then ask:

- "What does a word like <u>pip</u> become when reversed?" (Answer is <u>pip</u>)

- "What does a sentence like <u>up</u> <u>pop</u> become when reversed?" (Answer is <u>pop</u> <u>up</u>)

Technique: The Gap Game

This game is played to develop insight into word formation. The teacher could start with an example of how to play the game by saying:

- "Lets look at the word pat."
- "If we replace p by a gap it will look like _ a t and many words can come to mind, like fat, sat, and mat."
- "If we replace a by a gap we get p _ t and other words come to mind like pit, pet, and pot."
- "If we replace t by a gap we get pa _ which brings to mind pass, pad, and pam."
- "Now lets play this game with the following words…"

As long as this game is interesting to all, you can play this game for hours just starting with any word already met and creating a gap for which perhaps there is more than one answer. Of course, only expect the gap to be filled by sounds already met. If they have not met m, don't introduce the examples pam or mat.

The Gap Game Demonstrates:

- That signs can be taken out of words, from any place, and the words can still be developed by the learners;
- That the student's image of words is flexible enough so that an incomplete pattern can bring about a number of answers;
- That the same word can provide answers to a number of differently formulated questions;
- That not all questions have the same number of answers. There is no obligation to start with the first column; any example can be a starting point.

Technique: The Transformation Game

This game creates a new word from a given word. It is one that children and adults enjoy very much after they have become familiar with the rules. The object of the game is to go from one word to another through a succession of changes, using only four operations, and making only one change at a time:

- (s) substitution (of one sound for another)
- (a) addition (of one sound at the beginning or end of a word)
- (i) insertion (of one sound within a word)
- (r) reversal (of the sounds of a word)

The basis for the game is not single letters but signs, each of which may contain several letters representing one sound. Each step must produce a legitimate English word. In most cases, there is more than one way to go from one word to another.

(Note that subtraction is not permissible in the game, although it is obvious that it can be used for word formation. It would reduce the interest of the game by making almost all challenges much too easy.)

Transformation Game Examples:

Example 1: from <u>at</u> to <u>sips</u>

$$at \nearrow^{s} it \xrightarrow{a} pit \xrightarrow{r} tip \xrightarrow{a} tips \searrow^{s}$$
$$\searrow^{a} pat \xrightarrow{r} tap \xrightarrow{s} tip \xrightarrow{s} sip \nearrow^{a} sips$$

Example 2: from up to tests

```
              s       s       r      s       i       a
            sup  →  sip  →  tip  →  pit  →  pet  →  pest  →  pests
         ↗ o                                                        ↘ s
up                                                                       tests
         ↘ o                                                        ↗ s
             a       s       s      s       s       i
            ups  →  sups →  sips →  sits  →  sets →  pets  →  pests
```

These exercises correspond to what we did as babies when we first learned to speak. It truly reflects the functionings of the mind. You can easily recognize this when listening to young children play with sounds — they make many words from just a few sounds, then they learn to create different words by changing the order of sounds and adding new ones. These exercises are some of the most effective techniques available to support the development of reading skills from basic to advanced.

The game of transformations enhances this awareness and prepares students to retain the written form of words.

Give your student pairs of words for the game of transformation. Increase the difficulty and complexity of the challenges as the game develops.

You can introduce transformations after your student has completed the study of Primer Book R_1. The exercise can be worked out orally or in writing. Starting with pat, ask them: "How would this word sound with the "ice blue" one instead of the "buff" one?" (pet). Then ask him what other changes he can make (one at a time) to arrive at pits.

In the beginning don't insist on getting results, but rather make sure that the rules are clear and that your student understands what they are supposed to do. The transformation game is played throughout the Words in Color program. You can go back to it and present new challenges whenever you see that your student needs this type of exercise or wants to play the game.

Technique: Reading Upside-down

A good way to test decoding skills of the student is to have him or her read the words and sentences upside-down. This should only be done with words and sentences that they have already mastered since it will test their ability to know what is the correct orientation of the spellings and which direction to read.

A way to make this more fun is to time them while they attempt various sentences.

Technique: Point, Show, Engage

This is typically used in the earlier stages for beginning readers to get them acquainted with the conventions of reading.

Variation 1 Example:
Using the single signs <u>a</u> and <u>u</u> tap in rhythm (for example, <u>aa u</u>) and ask your student:

- "What did I show?"
- "What would the reverse of this be?"
- "Tap it yourself on the Fidel."

Variation 2 Example:
Point to one of the "words" in the Primer books and ask your student to read it. Then ask:

- "What would the reverse of this be?"
- "Is it written on this page?" yes? no?
- If yes, "Can you find it and show it to me?"

Technique: For Awareness of Spelling

We can indicate the spelling of words by moving or tapping the pointer from sign to sign. This enables the student to understand that the order of the letters corresponds to how the words are spoken.

For example, if you want the student to say the word <u>pat</u>, you would tap the pointer on each letter in order on the Fidel or on the word chart:
<u>p</u> <u>a</u> <u>t</u>

For students who have come to think of spelling mainly as the individual letters, awareness of the sounds in words can be renewed by separating these two activities when the work on the more difficult levels of spelling begins: first pointing to the sequence of columns, and then during a second pointing finding the exact sign in each column required for correctly spelling a particular word.

Example:

Initially, the teacher can point to an entire column where the sound exists. Below, it is indicated by tapping from 1, to 2, then 3.

a	u	i	y	e	o	a	e	u	o	a	o	e	a	oo	o	I	a	o	u	ou
au	o	o	ey	ea	a	u	o	o	a	ea	oo	ee	ai	ou	a	i	ai	oe	ew	hou
ai	a	a	ay	a	ho	i	ou	o	au	ah	ew	ea	ea	u	au	y	ay	ow	iew	ow
i	ou	u	ee	u	oh	io	oi	i	aw	aa	ou	y	e	o	oa	ie	ey	owe	eau	ough
	oo	e	ai	ai	ow	iou	oa	ea	owe	au	ui	ie	ei		oo	ye	ei	oa	ue	
	oe	ia	ei	ay	eau	eou	eo	ou	ough	e	u	ei	hei		ou	igh	eigh	ou	ieu	
		ie	hi	ie		ia	oi	y	oa		oe	i	ae		ho	eye	ea	ew	ewe	oi
		ea	hea	eo		ie	ei		augh		ue	eo	aye	eu	ao	eigh	aigh	oh	hu	oy
		ae	ois	ei		au	iu		oo		eu	ey	ayo	ue	oi	is	et	ough	eu	aw
		is		ae		ea	eau		ou		ough	ay	ey		owa	ais	ae	eau	eue	
						ah	ough		hau		wo	oe				ei	au	oo		
						he	y		ho		ieu	ae				aye	e	au		oi
									ao			is					ee	eo		
									oi									ot		o
									owa											

p	t	s	s	s	m	n	f	v	d	th	th	y	l	w	k	r	b	h	g	sh	ch	ng	j	qu	x
pp	tt	ss	ss	z	mm	nn	ff	f	dd	the	the	i	ll	wh	kk	rr	bb	wh	gg	ch	tch	n	g	cqu	xe
pe	te	se	se	ge	me	ne	fe	ve	de		h	j	le	u	ke	re	be	j	gu	t	t	ngue	d		cc
ph	ed	's	's	t	mb	kn	ph	lve	ed		t		lle	o	ck	wr	bu		gh	s	c	nd	dge		xc
bp	d	z	c		lm	gn	gh	ph	ld		phth		'l		c	rh	pb		gue	ss	che		ge		
	tte	zz	ce		gm	pn	lf	ve	'd						cc	rps			ckgu	c			gg		x
	pt		sc		mn	mn	ft		t				l	wh	ch	rp				sch			dg		
	bp		st		'm	gne	ffe		tt				'll		lk	rt				sc			dj		x
	ct		s			in	pph								qu	rrh				che					
	cht	thes				on									que	lo				chs					x
	th	sth			m	dne									cqu	re									
	phth	s'	sse			nd									cch	r									
	't		sth			ln									co	re									
	z	's	z			n									kh	re									
	zz																								

Then on a second pass, point to the exact sign corresponding to the letters:

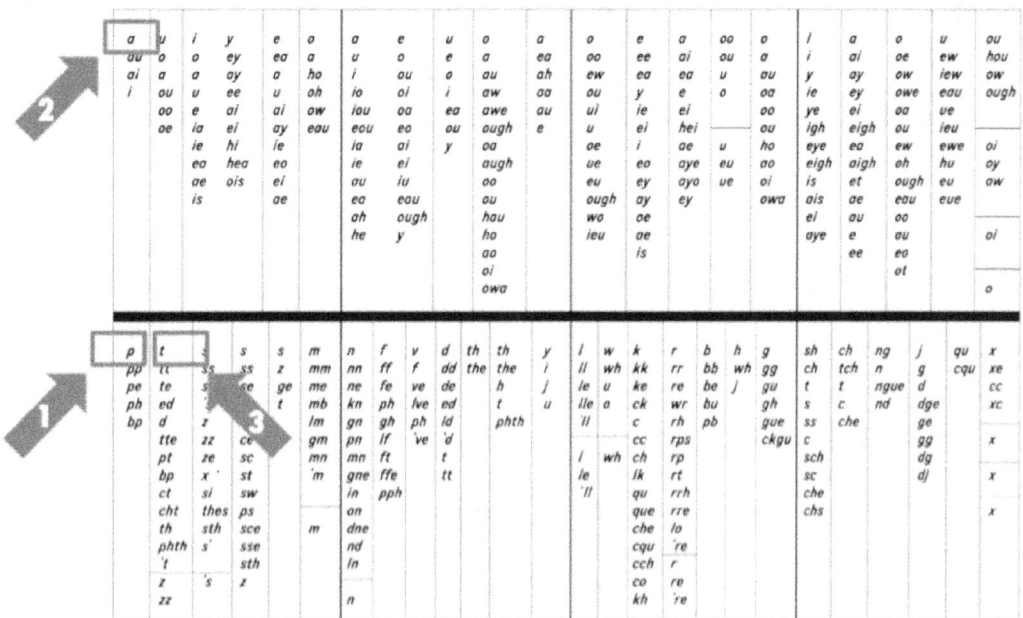

Note: this technique is used in both Visual, and Oral Dictation for individual/small groups/classrooms

If you are using Words in Color in a small group or larger classroom:

- It is suggested that the person tapping stands to the side of the charts as to not obstruct the view of others
- Allow other students to participate by asking individuals to go through the exercises
- If students are imprecise with their pointing, the teacher can ask; "Can you be more exact? I am not clear what you are showing"
- In situations where the correct spelling is important, the teacher could say: "For the sake of spelling, lets use these…. signs."

Technique: For Criteria and Autonomy

Ask a student, possibly the most advanced, to say each of the sounds as the teacher taps them out. (Oral Dictation)

The exercise can be reversed – i.e. the teacher says the sounds and one of the students points them out.

Then, ask the other students in the class to participate in determining whether the columns and the specific signs within the columns are being spoken or tapped correctly.

The doubts expressed by the students are examined and proper changes are made as required with regard to columns or signs within a column.

Instead of directly correcting them, students should be given opportunities to correct their own and one another's mistakes. Use probing questions or commands such as:

- "Are you sure you said it right?"
- "Are you 100% sure?"
- "Say it again."
- "Did he point it out correctly?"
- "Did she say it correctly?"
- "What is different between what was spoken and what was pointed out?"

This technique allows students to learn to choose correctly through the process of elimination and to take responsibility for their learning. It also allows students to take care of mistakes consciously, while working in a cooperative spirit.

Technique: Active Visualization for Retention

In order to actively involve students' power of evocation, we suggest that students close their eyes and note if they can mentally develop a whole word which corresponds to the words they have shown on the Fidel, Word Charts or have seen somewhere else.

This technique generates self-reliance in students and prepares them to feel confident when they are right.

For example, after a student taps out a word, the teacher might say:

- "Close your eyes."
- "Can you see the word?"
- "If not open your eyes and take a look at it."
- "Now close your eyes again, can you picture it?"
- "It is clear? Do you have a strong picture?"
- "If not open your eyes and take a look again."
- "Lets try again, close your eyes and see it in detail."

In this way, difficult words, or pairs of words that have some similar attributes can be examined, and processed thoroughly.

Technique: Writing

The next activity is to let students write down, on paper or on the chalkboard, the words they have formed on the Fidel and evoked in their minds.

It can be fun for students to exchange their notebooks, to read what others have written, and to discuss the correct way of writing words and showing them on the Fidel.

Since students meet the words again and again in the course of various learning activities — such as pointing out, evoking, writing down, and reading back — the drudgery of repetition is avoided.

These techniques also give continuous feedback, which allows teachers to evaluate all the time the learning taking place.

Soon after beginning to use the Fidel, teachers and students can make the observation that the signs given at the top of the columns occur in a number of words while less and less frequent spellings appear lower down in the columns. Presenting the whole of the Fidel gives students a sense of the way their language behaves, awakens their curiosity and maintains their interest in what they have yet to learn.

Technique: Introducing a New Sound

The student may be able to read certain words on the charts which you did not introduce through a formal method. Ask them to point and say a word they recognize on the Word Charts. For example, your student may know the word <u>let</u> because they have read it somewhere before. At this stage the student has been formally introduced to the <u>e</u> and <u>t</u> sounds, but not the <u>l</u>. Now is a good time to introduce the 'bright blue' <u>l</u> sound in column 41. Since this is a consonant, we can not say its sound in isolation. Instead, combine this new sound with ones the student already knows. Move to the Fidel and for example, tap out <u>l</u>, <u>a</u> and <u>p</u> to spell <u>lap</u>.

If the student is unable to read new words on the Word Chart, then move over to the Fidel, point to a new column and say it once. Then, point to it again, and have the student say it. Remember, if it is a consonant you must combine it with a vowel sound.

Technique: Introducing a New Spelling

If you want to introduce a new spelling to the student, you may find the following technique useful. For example, if your students know the word <u>fan</u> and the word <u>let</u>, they have been given enough criteria for them to accurately spell the word <u>laugh</u>.

Start by separately tapping out the words <u>fan</u> and <u>let</u> on the Word Charts. If they have trouble saying either of those words, slow down and do it again. When they get it, go to the Fidel and tap the individual symbols of <u>fan</u> (<u>f</u> <u>a</u> <u>n</u>) and then <u>let</u> (<u>l</u> <u>e</u> <u>t</u>). Now, tap on the same <u>l</u> (as in <u>let</u>), the <u>a</u> (as in <u>fan</u>) and the <u>f</u> (as in <u>fan</u>). Have them say <u>laf</u>.

Now introduce the correct spelling of <u>laugh</u>. Tap on <u>l</u> (as in <u>let</u>), then under the same column in the Fidel as the a (as in fan), tap on the au spelling, then tap the f (as in fan). You have tapped out lauf. Make sure the student pronounces the word the same as before. Repeat the process, this time tap the gh in the same column instead of the f. Repeat the process, if your students are having difficulty reading the word laugh.

This exercise can be done for a wide range of new words. For words that are not on the Word Charts, you will be able to tap all the spellings in the English language using the Fidel.

Technique: Introducing Diphthongs

A diphthong is formed by combining two sounds into one spelling. To see an example of one, look at column 16 on the Fidel. This column introduces a sound as in the first person I. As you can see this is combines the 'white' sound as in pot (column 5) with the 'pink' sound as in yes (column 40). Here is a technique which you may find useful when introducing these sounds.

Have the student find a word that has the 'white' sound, for example pot. Cover up the letter t only; the student should say po, cover up the p only; the student should say ot. Now, cover up both the p and the t until the student can isolate and pronounce the 'white' o properly. Now, move onto a word that has the 'pink' y, for example yes. Since the letter y in this word is a consonant, we can not pronounce it in isolation. Instead, tap the 'white' o, then tap the word yes. Have them say o-yes again until it sounds smoothly. Now, repeat this exercise, but this time cover the es. The student should be able to realize that he or she is blending the 'white' sound with the 'pink' sound together. They should be able to say the sound of the first person I. Have them repeat it until they say it smoothly with confidence. Now, you can introduce the correct spelling of the first person I by taping on it in column 16.

Technique: For Awareness of Blends

We have found that some beginning, or very young readers struggle with word blends or combining syllables.

For example, if you are trying to help your student go from the syllables pa and ap to the word pap, or from the syllable pa and at to the word pat, the following technique may be helpful.

The teacher would tell students:

- "Take this sound pa and put it in this hand (the left hand) and make a fist."
- "Take this sound ap, put it in the other hand (right hand) and make a fist."
- "What do you have in this hand (the left one)?"
- "What do you have in the other one (the right one)?"
- "Say this one (the left one), now say the other one (the right one)."
- "Now lets take our hands and put them close together – say the sounds in each hand."
- "Now let's put our hands closer still – say the sounds."
- "Next let's put them right beside each other – say the sounds."
- "Now let's clap our hands together – how do we say the sound now?"

At this point some students may pause to think through how they would say the sound. It is important that you give them time to work it out. If they don't immediately get it or if they give up, it is suggested that you do not give the answer to them. Rather, try the exercise again. A second time through might trigger something which leads to an awareness of how to pronounce the sound.

This technique can be used with other sounds, and in different orders. For example:

- pa and at → pat
- ta and ap → tap

Games

Games That Make The Fidel A Friend

All these games foster students' powers of perception, imagery, recall, and recognition. Retention takes place because the human capacities (e.g. perception, analysis, synthesis, abstraction, etc.) that enable learning are mobilized. Students are able to learn to be good spellers by being actively involved in their learning and thus do not need to rely on memorization.

As you and your students work with the Fidel, you will likely discover many more ways of using it.

Level One

For helping students learn the sound/sign correspondence

Level Two

Moving toward the complex spellings, and words of several syllables using almost all sounds

Level Three

For working on:

- 'long' words
- words with different signs representing the same sound
- words with the same signs representing different sounds

Level Four

For considering commonly used words which are exceptional in terms of their spelling because of their choice of letters for a particular sound

Game 1: Level 1

Teachers can prepare a list of common words using only the first spelling in a number of columns.

The teacher may form one of these words by pointing it out on the Fidel. For example: <u>an</u>. Next the teacher would present the students the challenge of forming as many words as they can with that word as part of them.

- <u>an</u>   <u>an</u>d, s<u>an</u>d, st<u>an</u>d, b<u>an</u>, b<u>an</u>d, h<u>an</u>d, <u>an</u>t, t<u>an</u>, p<u>an</u>t, p<u>an</u>ts, etc.

Another example might be:

- <u>it</u>   s<u>it</u>, p<u>it</u>, b<u>it</u>, l<u>it</u>, m<u>it</u>, k<u>it</u>, etc.

Game 2: Level 1

The same set of words can be used in a slightly different way. Students can be asked to start with a given word and to transform it into other words. Unlike the Transformation Game, the end point is not given.

For example:

- <u>on</u>   n<u>ot</u>, p<u>ot</u>, p<u>ots</u>, <u>spots</u>, <u>stops</u>, etc.
- <u>ten</u>   <u>tent</u>, <u>sent</u>, <u>spent</u>, <u>spend</u>, etc.
- <u>up</u>   p<u>up</u>, <u>pump</u>, <u>pumps</u>, <u>mumps</u>, etc.

The techniques mentioned before of forming words by pointing out on the Fidel, helping one another in the activity, evoking the words, writing them down, and reading what others have written, are all part of these exercises as well as of the ones that follow.

Game 3: Level 1

Phrases, and later sentences, may be formed containing little words given by the teacher or other students.

For example:

- is it / it is / as it is / is it as it is
- a man / a sad man / dad is a sad man
- as ten men sat in the tent, sam sent tom in

Note: In playing this game the unstressed sound of the sixth vowel column ('schwa') needs to be used in the words a and the.

a	u	i	y	e	o	a	e	u	o	a	o	e	a	oo	o	I	a	o	u	ou
au	o	o	ey	ea	a	a	o	e	a	ah	oo	ew	ea	ou	a	y	ai	oe	ew	hou
ai	a	ay	a	ho	i	ou	o	au	aa	ew	ea	ai	u	oa	ie	ay	ow	iew	ow
i	ou	u	ee	a	oh	o	oi	i	aw	au	ou	y	e	o	oo	ye	ei	oo	owe	eau	ough
	oo	e	oi	ai	ow	io	oa	ea	awe	e	ui	le	ei		ou	igh	ei	ou	oa	ue
	oe	ia	ei	ay	eau	iou	eo	ou	ough		u	ie	hei		u	eye	eigh	ew	ou	ieu
		ie	hi	ie		eou	ai	y	oa		oe	ei	ae		ho	eigh	aigh	oh	ewe	oi
		ea	hea	eo		ia	ei		augh		ue	eo	aye		ao	is	et	ough	hu	oy
		ae	ois	ei		ie	iu		oo		eu	ey	ayo	eu	ve	ai	au	eau	eu	aw
		is		ae		au	eau		ou		ough	ay	ey		oi	ais	ae	oo	eue	
						ea	ough		hau		wo	oe			owa	ei	au	ou		oi
						ah	y		ho		ieu	ae				aye	e	au		
						he			ao			is					ee	eo		o
									oi									ot		
									owa											

p	t	s	s	s	m	n	f	v	d	th	th	y	l	w	k	r	b	h	g	sh	ch	ng	j	qu	x
pp	tt	ss	ss	z	mm	nn	ff	f	dd	the	the	i	ll	wh	kk	rr	bb	wh	gg	ch	tch	n	g	cqu	xe
pe	te	se	se	ge	me	ne	fe	ve	de		h	j	le	u	ke	re	be	j	gu	t	t	ngue	d		cc
ph	ed	's	's	z	mb	kn	ph	lve	ed		t	u	lle	o	ck	wr	bu		gh	s	c	nd	dge		xc
bp	d	c	c	t	im	gn	gh	ph	ld		phth		'll		c	rh	pb		gue	c	che		ge		
	tte	zz	ce		gm	pn	lf	've	'd						cc	rps			ckgu	sch			gg		x
	pt	ze	sc		mn	mn	ft		t				l	wh	ch	rp				sc			dg		
	bp	x	st		'm	gne	ffe		tt				le		lk	rt				che			dj		x
	ct	si	sw			in	pph						'll		qu	rrh				chs					
	cht	thes	ps			on									que	lo									x
	th	sth	sce		m	dne									che	're									
	phth	s'	sse			nd									cqu	r									
	't		sth			ln									cch										
	z	's	z												co	re									
	zz					n									kh	're									

Game 4: Level 2

Students can now be asked to work on more difficult words in which one sign is composed of two letters representing one sound or multisyllabic words.

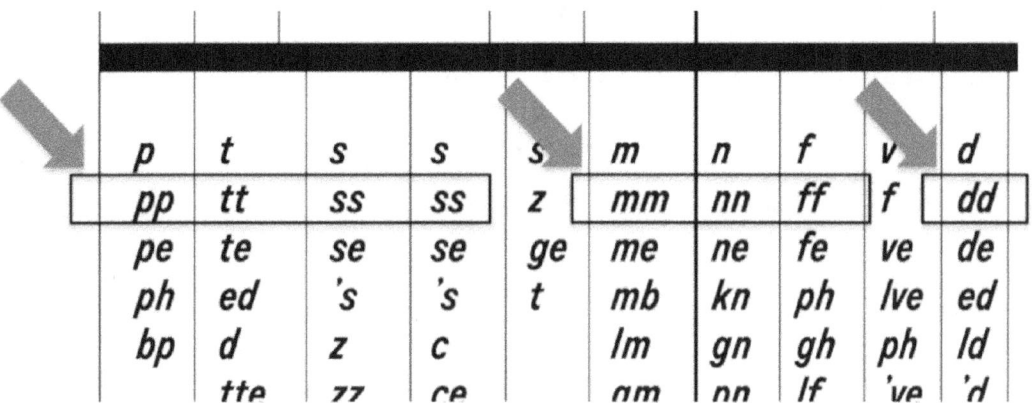

We can now insist that students listen to the number of beats they utter in a spoken word, and take note of the ones they stress and unstress.

Careful listening can help students close the gap between their spoken speech and to the actual sound they give to the vowel with each beat.

For example:

The teacher can say a word, such as, "<u>stops</u>" and then asks:

- "How many sounds do you hear?"
- "How many beats do you hear?"

The teacher can say two words, such as, "<u>stops</u>" and "<u>pots</u>" and then ask:

- "How many sounds in the first word? In the second?"
- "Which sounds are unique/different? Which sounds are similar?"
- "How many beats in the first? In the second?"

After working on simple words, the exercise can be extended to more complex words. In linking their speech to written signs by means of the Fidel, they can make sequences like:

- stop, stops, stopped, stopping, stopper
- tempt, tempted, tempting, attempt, attempted, attempting
- puppet, asset, assist, assistant, insistent
- stamps, stamped, stampede, stammer
- will, willing, willingly, unwillingly
- other, mother, brother, another

Game 5: Level 2

Sentences using words of this level of difficulty can now be orally dictated, and students asked to hold the entire sentence, as a whole, in their minds. They can then take turns pointing the sentences out on the Fidel.

Also, sentences can be pointed out on the Fidel (visual dictation) and students asked at the end of this pointing to say each sentence and then write it down.

For example:

- my brother will come willingly
- the man stamped a letter
- in the stampede at the match he lost her

Note:

If you are using Words in Color in a small group or larger classroom:

When the students have written down a number of such sentences they can exchange their books and/or read aloud the sentences. They can use their own criteria to see if there are any misspelled words and may consult the Fidel if they need to.

Game 6: Level 3

Words and sentences can now be proposed by the teacher, and the students, which exemplify certain characteristics and are interesting in terms of their meaning and usage.

For example:

- similar, similarity, simultaneous, simulate, simulation
- scent, century, central, sentinel, sententious,
- conscious, delicious, sufficient, deficient, efficient
- cushion, concentration, commission, physician

Examples using sentences:

- The sententious priest was central to the events of the century.
- He was conscious of the delicious taste but found the scent sufficient.
- Sitting on a cushion at the commission, the physician told of the concentration needed when operating.

Game 7: Level 3

After students have had sufficient practice on all of these levels to feel comfortable on the Fidel, teachers can ask them to produce their individual lists of words and attempt to use these words in sentences.

This activity can be guided by the teacher and the challenge made progressively more difficult.

Students may be asked to prepare lists:

- of one-syllable words they know for sure how to spell correctly
- of multi-syllabic words they feel sure of spelling correctly
- of words they utter aloud and, after carefully listening to their own voices write down — underlining those signs they are unsure about

Students may be given one, two, or three of these words to use together in one sentence. As they do so, they can be challenged to examine what part is played by the various meanings of the words when they are linked together in the same sentence.

If using Words in Color in a small group or larger classroom:

Students can take turns pointing out their words on the Fidel while others read them aloud and determine as a group which are the correct signs.

New lists can be prepared containing words common to the lists. Students may be struck by some of the words on other people's lists and may be encouraged to include them in their lists.

Game 8: Level 4

Hunting and collecting words with similar characteristics can be done by students individually or working in groups, at school and at home. Teachers would prepare the characteristics and students would then find words that met the criteria.

For example:

Find more words that fit with the words shown in each of the following groups words...

- <u>iron</u>, <u>fire</u>, <u>sapphire</u>, <u>giraffe</u>, etc.
- <u>colonel</u>, <u>lieutenant</u>, <u>sergeant</u>, etc.
- <u>catarrh</u>, <u>hemorrhage</u>, etc.
- <u>stereophonic</u>, <u>diaphragm</u>, <u>elephant</u>, <u>photograph</u>
- etc.

More Games

These games can be introduced at any of the preceding levels

Game 9: Any Level

The teacher picks a word in his or her head. He or she points out all signs except one; touch the wall above the Fidel to represent this "gap" and let the student point out what the missing sound with its appropriate sign could or should be.

For example:

- p __ t → could be pat, pet, pot, etc.
- st __ p → could be step, stop, etc.
- thr __ → could be through, throw, etc.
- __ t → could be at, it etc.

The same can be done with sentences leaving out one or two words.

- is it ___? → could be it is pat?, is it hot?, etc.
- it is ___. → could be it is hot. it is cold., etc.

There may be multiple answers, the key is for the student to have fun while exploring the language.

Game 10: Any Level

Reclassify words into groups on the basis that a part of the written form belongs to all of them and thus, in some way, makes them look alike even though they are not in any way related in meaning.

For example:

1. ill

    - pill, till, sill, mill, chill, spill,
    - skill, frill, quill, illustrate
    - illiterate, etc.

2. old

    - told, bold, sold, gold, cold, hold,
    - behold, unfold, soldier, etc.

3. ate

    - late, fate, pate, plate, state, hate,
    - crate, gate, dictate, inflate, translate,
    - frustrate, operate, irritate,
    - educate, concentrate, private,
    - pirate, climate, chocolate, etc.

4. ode

    - mode, bode, rode, strode, erode, corrode,
    - code, cathode, decode, explode, episode,
    - modeling, etc.

5. able

    - cable, table, stable, unstable,
    - reasonable, acceptable, educable,
    - penetrable, permeable, irritable, etc.

6. low

- slow, flow, glow, blow, below, billow,
- pillow, willow, hollow, follow, fellow,
- yellow, mellow, plow, flower, etc.

Game 11: Any Level

Group words for special reasons, such as:

- Words whose spelling is affected in a similar way when various endings are added. For example:
  - fun, funny, funnies
  - stop, stopped, stopping
  - write, written / bite, bitten
  - try, tries / dry, dries / carry, carries

- Pairs of words whose spellings are similar when one is formed from the other even though they sound different. Knowing the spelling of the first helps one in spelling the second. For example:
  - democrat → democracy   critic → criticize
  - confident → confidential   office → official
  - erudite → erudition   music → musician
  - fast → fasten   haste → chasten
  - limber → limb   muscular → muscle
  - signal → sign → design

- Words that are all connected in origin and have consistent ways of changing their spelling (and sometimes their sounding) when one is generated from the other. For example:
  - image, imagery, imaging, imagine, imagines,
  - imagined, imagination, imaginary, imaginable,
  - imaginative, unimaginatively

- Words that sound alike but have different meanings and spellings (homonyms). For example:
  - no, know
  - new, knew
  - so, sew, sow
  - pear, pair, pare (pare a pair of pears)

- Words that have the same spelling but are different sounding and have different meanings (homographs). For example:
    - sow, sow (my sow pulls up what I sow)
    - wind, wind (when the wind blows I wind my clock)
    - content, content (he felt content with the content of his book)

Game 12: Any Level

Study each particular sign that is found in more than one column on the Fidel and list as many examples as possible of its various sound values.

For example: the spelling <u>ou</u>

r<u>ou</u>gh	courag<u>eo</u>us	c<u>ou</u>rage	c<u>ou</u>gh	s<u>ou</u>p	c<u>ou</u>ld	p<u>ou</u>r	s<u>ou</u>l	<u>ou</u>t
t<u>ou</u>ch	luxuri<u>ou</u>s	c<u>ou</u>rtesy	tr<u>ou</u>gh	tr<u>ou</u>pe	w<u>ou</u>ld	f<u>ou</u>r	sh<u>ou</u>lder	<u>ou</u>r
c<u>ou</u>sin						c<u>ou</u>rse		s<u>ou</u>r
c<u>ou</u>ntry								

Game 13: Any Level

Studying all the columns one at a time on the Fidel and finding as many examples as possible for the various signs within it.

For example:

- sh   shock, shoe, splash, wish
- ch   chef, machine, michigan, chamois
- t   action, generation, partial, pretentious
- s   sugar, sure, pension, expansion
- ss   tissue, obsession, pressure
- c   precious, appreciate, special
- sch   schist (British English schedule)
- sc   conscience, conscientious
- che   cache, moustache
- chs   fuchsia

This game can be played at first by studying examples of the top 2, 3, or 4 signs in each column — i.e. the common spellings — before trying to collect examples of the less frequently used signs found further down the columns.

www.ingramcontent.com/pod-product-compliance
Lightning Source LLC
Chambersburg PA
CBHW081830300426
44116CB00014B/2541